MILLENNIUM
Young people's
CONGRESS

Be the Change!

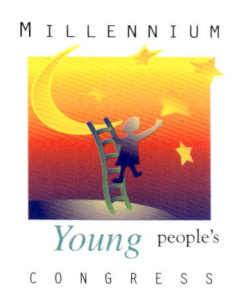

Youth solutions for the new millennium
"If you want to change the world, be the change!"

by
Young People of the World

Peace Child

ISLAND HERITAGE
PUBLISHING

Produced by
Peace Child International

www.peacechild.org

Congress Co-Director:

David Woollcombe

Maeona Mendelson

Editorial Consultant:

Donovan Slack

Designers:

José Luis Bayer

Ivonne Lacombe

Published by
ISLAND HERITAGE
PUBLISHING

A division of the Madden Corporation

99-880 Iwaena Street

'Aiea, Hawai'i 96701-3202

Fax: 808-488-2279

Phone: 808-487-7299

Email: hawaii4u@islandheritage.com

ISBN 0-89610-416-8

©2000 Peace Child International
& Island Heritage Publishing
All Rights Reserved. No portion of this book may be reproduced, modified or enhanced without prior written consent from Island Heritage Publishing. We thank Daniel Dubie and Geri Cvitanovich-Dubie at whose ranch on the North Shore, O'ahu, this book was assembled.

Printed in China.

MILLENNIUM
Young people's
CONGRESS

Be the Change!

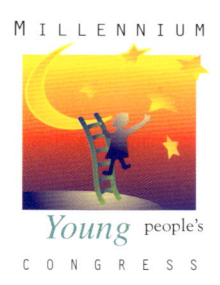

Youth solutions for the new millennium
Youth submission to the Rio + 10 Earth Summit Review, 2002

Editors

Dominique Mansilla Hermann
Argentina

Randolf Pinaya Perez
Bolivia

Michelle Luxon
Canada

Famara Singhata
The Gambia

Dhruv Malhotra
India

Solveige Skendelyte
Lithuania

Renza Moniz
Qatar

Mammen Tharakan
Qatar

Jelka Fric
Slovenia

Thomas Burke
United Kingdom

Adam Bien
Morgan Lee Woolley
Erin Mendelson
USA

Anusha Jogi
Zimbabwe

UNITED NATIONS · NATIONS UNIE

THE SECRETARY-GENERAL'S
MESSAGE TO THE MILLENNIUM YOUNG PEOPLE'S CONGRESS
Hawaii, October 24-28, 1999

I am pleased to send my best wishes to all of you gathered from around the world on the occasion of the Millennium Young People's Congress. Your commitment to building a better future for succeeding generations is an ideal which the United Nations shares with you.

As we approach the third millennium we should not forget that youth represents more than just a ready resource; young people have always stood for the hope that the mistakes of the past, our mistakes, will not be repeated. They offer us the prospect of redemption; that some of the damage we have done to this world can be repaired.

Perhaps youth can succeed where we have not yet triumphed. Perhaps our children can make a stronger commitment to the environment, to development, to peace and security than we have done. Perhaps they will, but I can assure you that it will be a far more difficult task if they live in isolation, if they do not experience other cultures and other traditions. More than anything, young people need to learn an important lesson that we have failed fully to grasp — despite our diversity, we are not all that different from one another. We share the same basic needs that people felt a thousand years ago and that people will continue to feel a thousand years from now: the need for safe water, shelter from violence, both natural and man-made; food for the family; a job; schooling for the children; and a state which does not oppress its citizens but rules with their consent.

There will of course be new challenges in the future, just as we today face challenges that did not exist fifty years ago. I believe that humanity, then as now, will require a forum in which states and other actors can come together to find the solutions. That is where the United Nations comes in. As a global institution, the UN is a place where people can come together to find global solutions to global problems.

That is also where gatherings such as yours come in. By meeting and discussing the problems which afflict our world today, you are laying a strong foundation for dealing with the problems that you and your children will face tomorrow. It is my hope that, after this meeting, you will continue to remain active in the battle against the despair and destitution that confront our world. And I hope that you will, in your time, keep the United Nations a strong and vital resource in your efforts. In that spirit, I wish you a successful congress.

Kofi A. Annan

Kofi Annan, Secretary General, United Nations

UNEP

I warmly welcome the Millennium Young People's Congress and its goal to promote the involvement of young people in Agenda 21 and enhance education for sustainable development into the next millennium.

Klaus Topfer, Executive Director,
United Nations Environment Program

Republic of Namibia
The President

I wish to register the support of the government and people of Namibia for the ideals and objectives of the Millennium Young People's Congress to be held in Hawaii.
The Congress shows that youth are seeking to become active in addressing problems that affect our planet.
I believe that young people must be provided with appropriate platforms where they can express their insights, their wishes, and their concern about the future of humanity.

Sam Nujoma,
President of the Republic of Namibia

I was delighted to meet the young delegates and activists from India to the Millennium Young People's Congress at Honolulu, Hawaii, in October 1999. I was impressed by their awareness and the eagerness to address issues that are of critical importance to the future of humanity and the world. The confidence and optimism with which young people all over the world face the future that belongs to them is indeed heartening.
I wish the organizers and the young participants of the Congress every success.

K. R. NAYAYANAN,
President of the Republic of India

unicef
United Nations Children's Fund

The objectives of the Congress are much in line with our own. One of our key program priorities is to promote young people's participation in activities that concern their present and future interests, including their own health, education, and the sustainable development of their communities and countries.

Carol Bellamy, Executive Director,
UNICEF

This Congress is an important opportunity to bridge the generation gap and to forge a new path into the next millennium. I believe strongly that, as senior leaders, we must extend our hand, share what we know and pass on the knowledge to young people because they hold the future of the world in their hands.

Senator Daniel Inouye, United States Senate, Chair, Millennium Host Committee

I consider this Congress an outstanding event to unite the young generation all over the world in the grand crusade to struggle for life and the fate of the earth. Mongolia, where 65% of the population are children and youth, attaches great importance to this Congress which provides a unique opportunity for their delegation to present the goals decided at their National Forum.

Rinchinnyam Amarjargal,
Prime Minister of Mongolia

Editors' Introduction

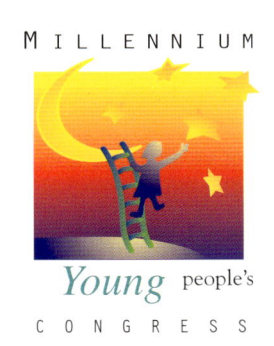

MILLENNIUM Young people's CONGRESS

It's been a long while since humans lived in a peaceful land without hunters. Our lives have changed completely and with them the environment surrounding us. Our challenge now is to redisover that harmony to sustain life through the next 1,000 years. That's what this Congress was all about.

Land without hunters

Alexander Schmidt, 12, Russia

Mana
is the Hawaiian word for
spirit—the power of the spirit. Leaders
have Mana—meaning presence, dignity, a
sense that they are worthy of respect and reverence. Works of art have Mana—a sense that in the
brushstrokes, the weave of a tapestry, or the lines of
a poem, a greater power is at work. We hope that,
through the pages of this book, you will feel the
mana of the many thousands of young people who put their energy into this
Congress

Human beings build airplanes, concoct vaccines that prevent diseases, build great cities, and compose dazzling works of art. But human beings also massacre each other and rape the natural world to the point where it is barely able to support life. Some experts say that we have a window of time—maybe ten, maybe fifty years—to set things right. That's our generation. Just by being here we either contribute to the problem or to the solutions. So we cannot sit idly watching the problems unfold before us: we must mobilize ourselves for the change that it is our generation's duty to put into action.

Some years ago, governments gathered in Rio de Janeiro for an Earth Summit. They produced Agenda 21, an action agenda designed to show how to save the planet and improve the lives of the world's poorest peoples at the same time. Peace Child produced a children's edition of this—and it was very good, but it was not the young people's own agenda. That's why we needed to do this Congress—to enable young people themselves to develop their own agenda; to determine their own priorities.

It began with thousands—millions!—of young people filling out priority cards and sending them to national coordinators. National meetings were held at which young people democratically voted for their top priorities and elected representatives to carry them to the Congress in Hawaii. Then 612 of us met in Hawaii to listen to each other, brainstorm, and set global strategies for dealing with the priorities we all agreed upon. We met with mentors who shared their valuable knowledge and experience, discussed every problem plaguing the earth, and eventually produced our top ten global priorities. Then we got down to business of reviewing the detailed action plans which each delegate submitted to address the priorities.

Education emerged as everyone's top priority for the new millennium. The youth expressed a thirst for the very thing that most adults assume we hate: SCHOOL! But, it is not school that we crave—it is a totally new kind of education that prepares us to live in harmony with our environment and each other. We desire an education that stimulates and engages our creative energies and applies validly to our lives—not the stifling schools that imprison us within four walls. Like many generations before us, we seek outlets for our energy, creativity, love, and devotion. The Congress helped us design an infrastructure to serve as a conduit through which our ideas may flow.

Why was Hawaii the perfect place for the Congress? It is a melting pot of many cultures whose representatives live the caring "spirit of aloha" which makes any stranger feel immediately at home. Also, we were inspired by stories of the Polynesian navigators who found Hawaii using only stars, faith, and intuition. We need the same kind of faith and intuition to chart our way through the next 1,000 years. And the youth of Hawaii invited us! They are exploring ways to return to sustainable lifestyles like the indigenous people of these islands lived for hundreds of years. It's the same sustainability we seek for our planet.

It was always the intention to produce this report. National coordinators collected tons of artwork, poems, essays, and action plans for this book. We, the editors, had just two weeks to put it together. We gathered on the North Shore of Oahu in a lush mountain retreat set in a rainforest with gorgeous palms, trees, and helpful mosquitoes! The poor little house barely survived the insane clatter of our typing, mass feedings, and general havoc. We endured sleepless nights, gallons of caffeine-packed tea and coffee, and tons of mosquito bites in order to bring you this book of the young people's priorities.

In it, we hope you will find evidence of young people's creativity and commitment. We know we cannot resign ourselves to gradual planetary devastation and human extinction. We hope this book will inspire and motivate you to think up and execute action proposals to address the priorities in your own life. As we cross into the next millennium, it is clear that we cannot expect change to just show up. We have to BE THE CHANGE!!!
                                                                The Editors

Contents

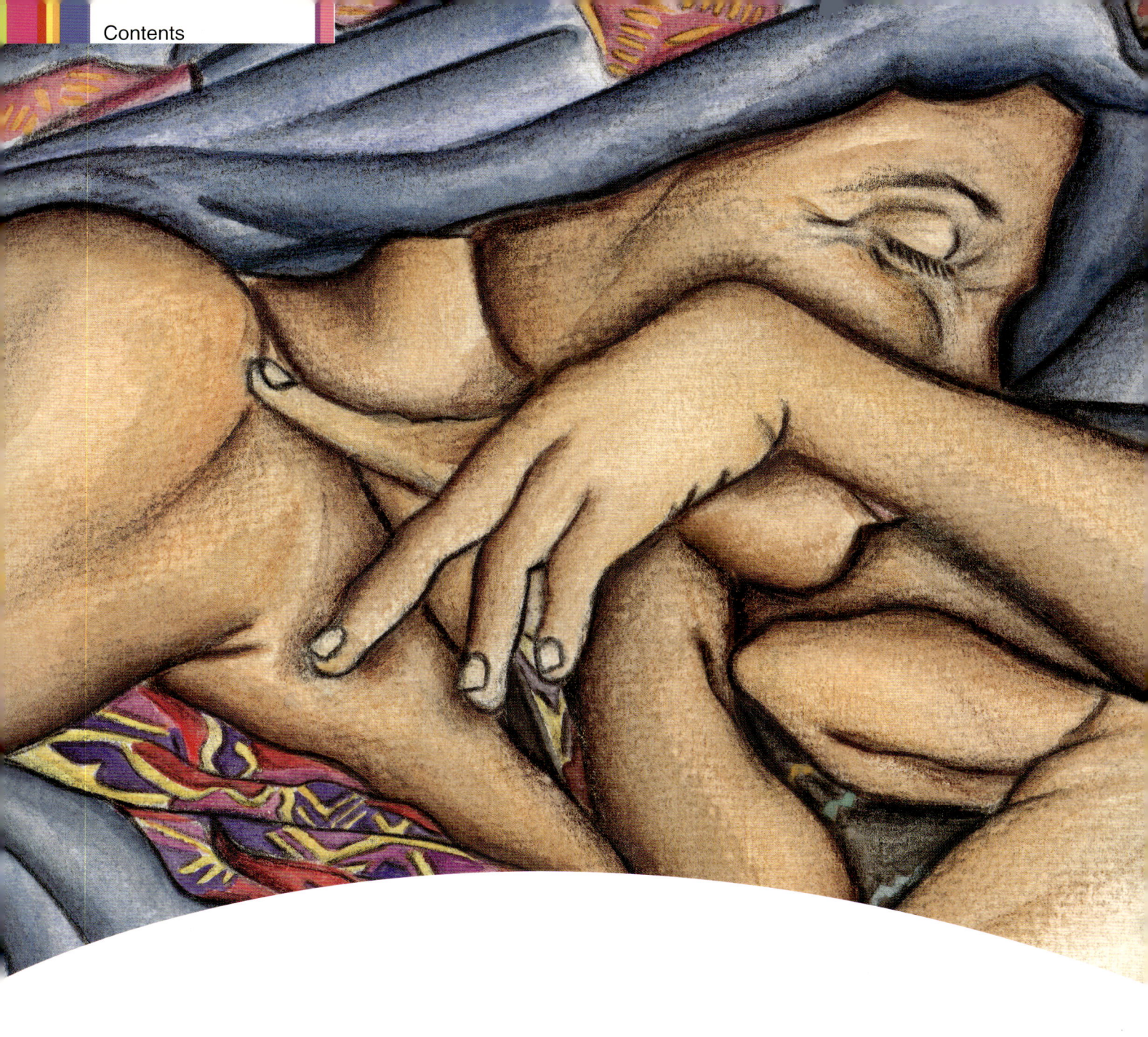

The Secretary-General's Message to the Millenium Young People's Congress; Messages from UNEP, UNICEF, the Presidents of Namibia, Senator Daniel Inouye, the President of India, and the Prime Minister of Mongolia; Editors Introduction;

6 - 9

Section I:
The Congress
National Consultations
Congress Diary
Peace Garden
Eco-Village

10 - 19

Section II:
Priorities & Action Plans
Education
Peace
Environment
Human Rights
Health
Poverty
Population

20 - 64

Renza Moniz, Qatar

Priorities & Action Plans
Corruption
Economy
Democracy
Animal Rights
Other Priorities
Substance Abuse

65 - 75

Section III: The Face of Change
U 'n Me: UN and Youth
Global Youth Assembly
Millenium Action Fund
Millenium Dialogues
Peace Child International

76 - 87

Reference
Acknowledgements
Regional Priorities

88 - 96

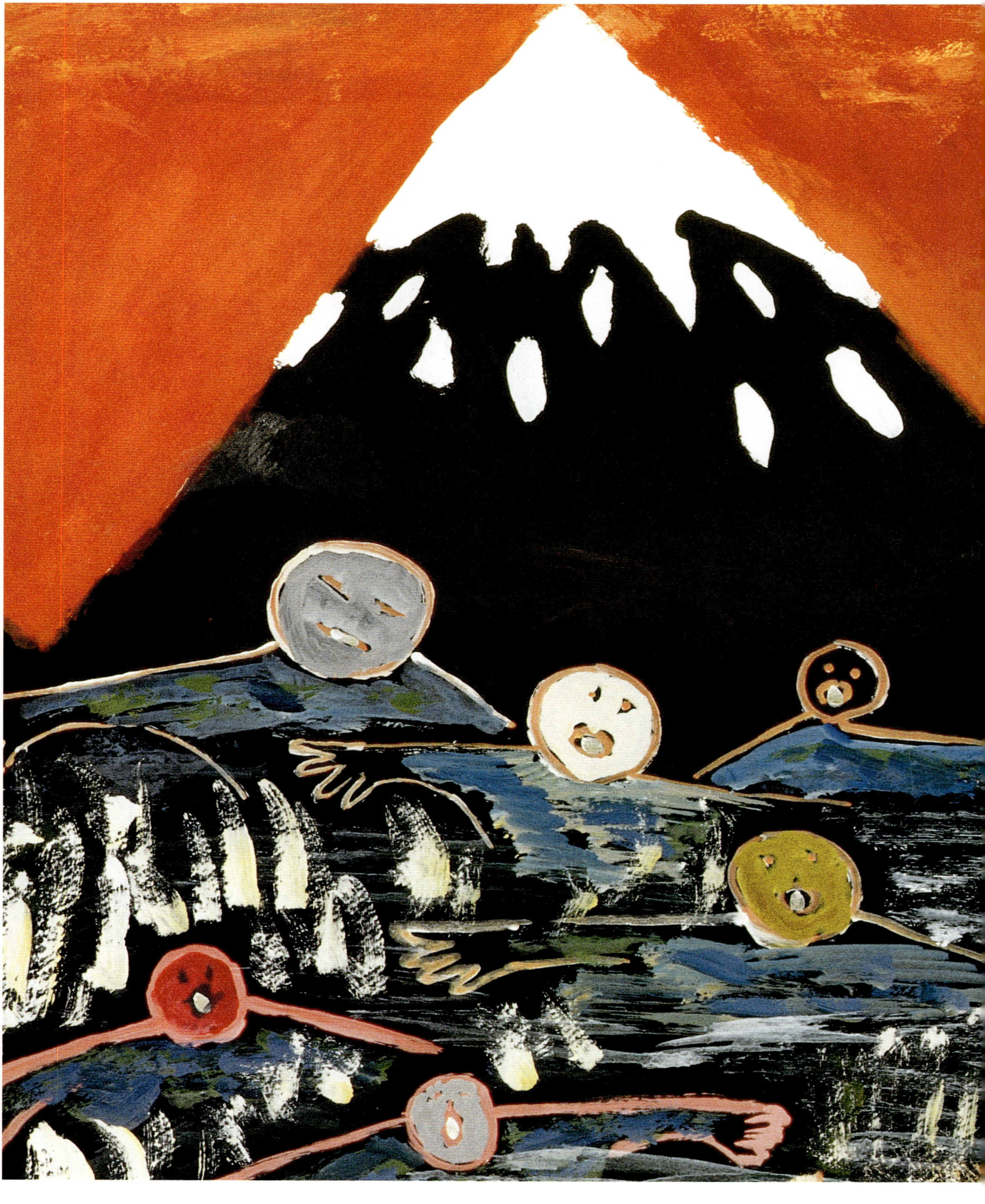

The Congress

National Consultations
Congress Diary
Peace Garden
Eco Activities

Youssef el Filali, Morocco

be the change

11

The Congress

National Consultations

Massive consultations preceded the Congress involving 15 to 20 million young people worldwide. Most of them were organized by young people. At each one, priorities were democratically selected and delegates were elected to present them in Hawaii. With no funding from the organizers, they had to rely on their own ingenuity and charm to pull them off—which, of course, they did magnificently. It was a truly youth-led event.

Qatar:

Dana Shaddad, our national coordinator, was only 15, but she organized us like one several times her age. She approached all the schools and got discussions going about our national priorities. Many sent in priority cards which we reviewed in our group, the Nature Preservers, deciding which to bring up at our big National Consultation. At that meeting, representatives from all the participating schools selected the top ten priorities. We then discussed the best solutions to them and set about crafting these into action plans to present to the Congress. We were going to Hawaii, much to the envy of our teachers and friends. But it was a lot of work! We had to find sponsors, get visas, organize flights. Hundreds of e-mails raced between Peace Child and Dana. Stress levels rose as the departure date approached and we still did not have enough sponsors. All of us slogged through the nights, writing letters, calling people. Finally we found enough money! The day of departure approached. Hawaii—here we come.   *Renza Moniz*

Slovenia:

Hawaii? Who is going to Hawaii? When I heard about the MYPC happening in Hawaii, I knew I wanted to be part of the team. From then on, I work very hard to finish my project to take to the National Consultation to convince them that I was a true activist. That took place in May. People sent in amazing drawings, paintings, poems, and project articles. We selected the best pieces of work and sent them to Peace Child to be used in the first draft of this book, which was circulated to all delegates and mentors. Then we democratically elected a team of judges to select two national delegates and one editor(me!!). Others who were not selected were invited to raise their own funds and seek selection as activists. Happily, the International Steering Committee at their meeting in July selected six more of us as activists. A team of nine was formed, and we set about preparing ourselves to play our role in this vital Congress to make the world a better place.   *Jelka Fric*

Gambia:

Mr. Buramindeh Kinteh invited several national youth organizations to a National Consultation meeting which brought together over 1,000 young people from all parts of the country and from different walks of life. Each organization came up with its own priorities to present to the meeting. After a heated but constructive discussion, we elected two delegates and selected our top five priorities: 1. teenage pregnancy; 2. baby dumping; 3. sexually transmitted diseases and AIDS; 4. coup d'etats and the abuse of human rights and democracy; 5. Girls education and violence against women. Tragically, despite an invitation from Hawaii Senator Daniel Inouye, the US embassy refused our elected delegates the visas to come to the Congress, so I, as a journalist with a multiple US entry visa, was appointed to bring the Gambian priorities and ideas to this Congress.
Famara Singata

by Ravin Thapa, Nepal

roximate locations of National Consultations

India:

The national coordinator, India for the MYPC was WWF-India. They conducted a rigorous selection process for the delegates. Priority cards were sent to all members of the Nature Clubs of India by the WWF education division. We had to list five priorities most vital to the sustaining of life in the new millennium. We also had to create poems, essays, articles, paintings, and cartoons to support and complement our priorities. After our submissions were screened by the regional divisions of WWF-India, the best entries were selected, and candidates were invited to express their views on the two priorities closest to their hearts in a speech or declamation. An esteemed panel of drama and media personalities was appointed to judge the declamations. After the regional heats, five to ten students were selected from each region to be interviewed by the WWF-India Heads of Department and some of the regional judges. After the interview, Juhi Nagarkatti and I were selected to represent our country. It was a moment of great pride for us to be appointed to carry the views of Indian youth to this global forum. Activists were selected in the same way. Each submitted an application highlighting their activities in social and environmental areas. The most active individuals were interviewed and nine were chosen. The Indian consultation involved more than 150,000 children from all over the country. All of us are grateful to have been allowed to contribute to this noble endeavour.

Dhruv Malhotra

Morocco:

With the support of his majesty, the late King Mohammed VI, the young people of Morocco enjoyed one of the most elaborate National Consultations of all. Schools in all parts of the country were invited to submit their priorities. Delegates from schools in all the major cities and many from rural areas gathered in the resort of Bouznika for the National Consultation. Peace and tolerance emerged as the top priorities, reflecting the ancient ideals of our country. Unemployment, poverty, civic morality, and access to technology were among the others democratically selected.

Young Reporters Group

Argentina:

Adults became the servants (slaves?!) of young people in the arrangement of many National Consultations. Here is the perspective of one of the many long-suffering parents dragged into the process:

Trying to have an adequate representation from a country as large as Argentina meant really hard work. Some of the participants came from 2,000 to 3,000 km away, so we had to think of accommodations, meals, and so on. I resigned myself to a week with my bedroom, kitchen, living room, and garden invaded by a horde of noisy young people—and not just me: all our friends, neighbors, and relatives were drawn in by the energy and motivation of Marina and her friends. That is what inspired us. Overall what impressed me most was the sense of democracy that all these youth had—especially encouraging for one of my generation. The election of the two national delegates was clearly and wholly democratic.

Each of the groups representing the different provinces had to propose a girl and a boy. Each candidate gave a speech to the audience expressing their current concerns, how they would solve them, and a reason for wanting to represent Argentina at the Congress. After hearing the eloquent speeches, the youth of Argentina cast their secret ballots and two excellent young people were chosen.

At the end of the consultation, I was filled with joy to see the fruits of our labor. This generation spoke out for themselves and chose their delegates with great intelligence and integrity. I could not have been more proud, for truly if young people create an experience of democracy for themselves in this way at this age, they will never allow the forces of dictatorship ever to take over our country again.

M. Susana Hermann de Mansilla, mother of Marina, 16, president of Rescue Mission Argentina

The Congress

Congress Diary

(None of our friends took us seriously when we said we were going to a hard-working Congress in Hawaii!! "Good excuse for a holiday!" they thought. Well, there was some of that, but just to show you how hard we DID work, here is a diary of the Congress:**)**

THURSDAY, OCTOBER 21

Aaargh! Jet lag! After traveling 24 to 48 hours, the delegates piled into the Honolulu airport, each feeling the vast hour differences in time. Back home, it was time to be sleeping; it was time to get up for school; it was noon the following day. However, they were quickly distracted by the beautiful landscapes, breath-taking sunsets, and warm, friendly faces.

Hawaiian Scenery - Sea Life Park

FRIDAY, OCTOBER 22

Sea Life Park was a glimpse of sustainability through marine biology and oceanography. For many, it was the first time ever to see dolphins, turtles, and seals up close. It was hot but a lot of fun!

SATURDAY, OCTOBER 23

We loaded the buses and sang all the way to the USS *Missouri* (Mighty Mo where the US-Japanese peace treaty was signed). We mingled and smiled emphatically while shouting "aloha!" as a helicopter hovered above and photographed us. Then we all got down to some hard work, painting murals or swabbing the decks of Mighty Mo or sweating on the edge of the Diamond Head crater building the Peace Garden. We broke language barriers and planted native Hawaiian plants as we united to building a permanent memory of the Congress. That evening, we danced the night away at a concert held on the cool beaches in front of the Hilton Hawaiian Village. It was a magnificent and exhilarating blend of cultural dances, beautiful languages, and new friendships.

Akahai is the Hawaiian word for kindness with an overarching sensation of tenderness. Akahai is the glue which holds families and friendships together - forgiving, compassionate, profoundly loving. We found a lot of akahai here in Hawaii.

SUNDAY, OCTOBER 24

After lots of photos and speeches, the Peace Garden was blessed by a Hawaiian priest who performed a traditional Hawaiian dedication ceremony. We placed "pohaku's" around a time capsule which contained vision statements from the Congress. Then we sang "We Are the World!" and thought about what we, the youth, could accomplish.

The bus experience

Planting trees

be the change
14

MONDAY, OCTOBER 25

We arrived at the beautiful state capitol building and sectioned into our regional groups. A wave of energy came over the building and the Congress began with some impromptu drumming and lively dancing which erupted in the Latin American region. Governor Benjamin Cayetano welcomed us and then we were off into our regional groups to discuss the priorities. Tension began to rise as each region discussed the definitions of the priority, its importance and it solutions. It was a long day—both frustrating and fun—but we managed to survive another day in Paradise. That night, the Opening Gala was held at the Hilton Hawaiian Village. The Morrocans, Zimbabweans, and Slovakians danced, and the Azerbajani boy sang his heart out as we cheered and danced along.

Regional meetings at the states capitol

TUESDAY, OCTOBER 26

Mentor Day: Mixed reviews— some were bored ("I'm glad I brought my postcards to write!"); some were inspired ("I never knew how important algae was to our world!"). Each mentor was invited to ask a question of the delegates. "What is the root cause of our problems?" asked Hanne Strong. Answer? "It is pollution - pollution of our minds, pollution of our spirits, and pollution of our environment through our excessive consumption..." Zehra Aydin told us that she often asked herself "What do I really want?" In answering that, you get good clues to who you really are as a person. Peter Raducha posed an interesting one: "Suppose Kofi Annan is surfing in Hawaii and gets wiped out by a huge wave; he's in the hospital for 30 days and you must fill in as Secretary-General of the UN. What would you do?" In the afternoon, we talked to the mentors in small groups. Most were extremely interesting and mind-stretching, but some were terminal bores.

Star mentors: Levar Burton and Hanne Strong

WEDNESDAY, OCTOBER 27

Today was the Day of Decisions. After meeting again in regional groups to finalise the top priorities, we moved into Inter-regional groups in which the representatives came together to compile the global priorities. Surprisingly, it was unanimous that Education was the top global priority for the new millennium!

HORMONES! Love is in the air!!!

When 612 people from around the world get together in one place, curiosity and hormones take over! We spent a lot of time mingling, sharing experiences, and exchanging smiles and winks.

The boys were overwhelmed by the diversity and international beauty surrounding them. Likewise, many girls were fascinated by the various looks, nationalities and physiques of these stunning young men!

In the spirit of the Congress's goals to unite, cooperate, and find collaborative solutions, boys and girls started to flirt, play hard to get, and pursue the friendships that will last long after they leave the island of paradise.

Make love, not war—it's cheaper and much more fun!!!

Jelka Fric, 18, Slovenia

be the change
15

The Congress

THURSDAY, OCTOBER 28

We gathered at the beautiful Hawaii Convention Center where we discussed our solutions to the priorities. Each country shared action plans and discussed ideas and proposals. Then we headed off to enjoy the serenity and beauty of Kualoa Ranch. We relaxed, chatted, and danced the night away in celebration of our achievements.

Friends

FRIDAY, OCTOBER 29

We released the outcomes of the Congress to an eager press. We also discussed how to network among each other. Most of us committed to be regional outreach officers that would promote the results of the Congress to our peers. Mia Handshin talked about the conference to take place in Australia next year. The night ended with a traditional Peace Child candle ceremony where we watched a thousand flames flicker in each other's eyes and sang "We shall overcome, shall live in peace, shall change the world!" Amid an emotional sea of tears and hugs and photograph flashes, we looked around at our new-found friends and knew that they would live in our minds and hearts forever.

Small group meetings

An afternoon of volleyball

Kyrghizstan holds forth

Morgan & Anusha - hard at work!

The editorial caucus

After one day of rest, it was off to Daniel Dubie's beautiful ranch on the North Shore of Oahu. The editors began their stressful process of assembling this book. We had to edit the long speeches and essays that young people had written about their priorities and sort through the wealth of wonderful poems, pictures and cartoons, making the agonizing selections of which to include and which to leave out. We were surrounded by magnificent statues of Buddha which cast their creative spirits on us as we brainstormed, and typed like mad. We survived the sleepless nights, gallons of tea and coffee, and endless mosquitoe bites and even found time to go to the beach! It was an experience that we will never forget and each editor has contributed their unique personality to make up a lovely and very memorable bunch. We have all become quite close and our efforts have united to bring you this book of the youth's global priorities.

The Editors

be the change
16

Aloha and mahalo to the host families

They got out of their car and ran toward me—a couple with two children carrying orchid leis. One kid gave me a hug and put the lei around my neck. I felt so welcome.

Next morning, I was woken by my little host sister who took me downstairs to watch her favorite cartoons. At that point, I felt like a member of the family. They gave me delicious meals (no junk food!), washed my clothes, took me on outings around the island. In everything, they gave me the feeling that I was at home. I know that every other delegate I spoke to had the same experience. So I would like to take this opportunity to thank all the families who took us into their homes and let us be a part of their lives. THANK YOU!!! We couldn't have made it without you!

Host family group

The editors' ranch

Buddhas all around!

Azerbaijani dancers

Star singer

John Devaraj, India, sings "Bananas"

Artists groups

One of the most inspiring parts of the Congress was the presence of different artists groups representing different cultures. They performed at the opening and closing night galas as well as the Rock Concert. Among them were dancers from Azerbaijan, Zimbabwe and Slovakia and a rap duo from Canada. Leading the Azerbaijan group was an extremely talented boy who was only 12-years-old. When he started singing "O sole mio" on the first night, the audience went crazy clapping hands and dancing. He was a fantastic performer! The Slovakian group amazed us with their adorable costumes (the girls looking as sweet as little dolls) and traditional dancing routines. Then we were treated to some Zimbabwe dancing. We loved their quick, lively rhythm and intricate costumes. The Canadians rounded things off with their rapping, dancing and singing! Not only did every group inspire us by giving us a piece of their heritage, they made us respect each and every culture in our world. Each one has so much of beauty and joy to offer us.

be the change

17

Peace Garden

Millennium Peace Garden

Youth for Environmental Service (YES) was the perfect group to be the Hawaiian partner for the Congress. With several important environmental projects under its belt, the YES focus was always going to be on action rather than words. So YES decided to get the Congress participants to get their hands dirty building a permanent memorial in Hawaii to the Congress. Sean Casey, executive director of YES, explains:

During the Congress, the youth constructed a Millennium Peace Garden on the slopes of Diamond Head. The construction of the garden took place in one day, October 24, 1999, on seven acres of degraded land. Under the supervision of YES, Rotary Club of Honolulu. and the planning committee, Congress participants built all the vital features of the garden including the installation of the irrigation system, moving stone and planting materials, and planting of the native Hawaiian plants.

Our goal was to demonstrate that a once degraded piece of unused land can be fully restored to a fully-functioning natural ecosystem. To this end, native Hawaiian plants, including Polynesia-introduced, indigenous, and endemic plants were planted throughout the garden.

The garden was designed with the help of students in coordination with the Peace Garden Advisory Committee, the Diamond Head Community Advisory Committee, PBR Hawaii, and the Hawaii State Department of Land and Natural Resources.

Community volunteers organized and supervised by the YES organization will maintain the garden.

Over the past two years, YES has been very successful in recruiting volunteers for restoration projects at Diamond Head. All told, YES has recruited more than 1,000 youth volunteers for Diamond Head projects. These volunteers have planted more than 800 native Hawaiian plants, removed over one ton of rubbish and other debris, and removed more than two tons of dead wood and plants that posed a fire hazard.

The Millennium Peace Garden is a highly public, international garden, elegantly demonstrating the principles of environmental sustainability and world peace.

For more information on YES and its programs, contact: www.yes1.org

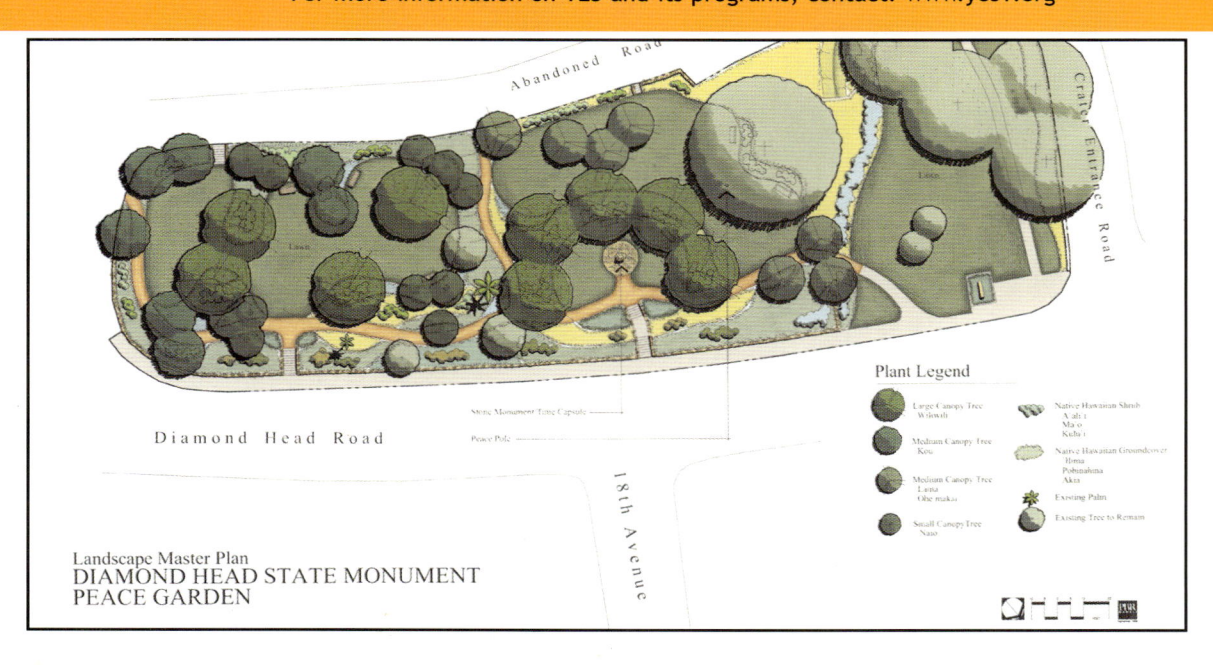

Landscape Master Plan
DIAMOND HEAD STATE MONUMENT PEACE GARDEN

Eco-Village

In Kaneohe, on the slopes of the Koolau Mountains in Ho'omaluhia Botanical Gardens, 18 international delegates and activists camped out in a village designed to demonstrate practical sustainability. They dodged rain showers and withstood the howling wind to survive nine nights without hot water and electricity in cabins built by the University of Hawaii School of Architecture. All agreed that this was one of the most successful aspects of the Congress.

The custom-built bungalows were constructed with recycled wood, natural bamboo, scraps of sails, and aluminum cans.

Promptly at 6:45 a.m. each day, everyone was pushed out of their hammocks, bunks, and lofts, and piercing cold showers started the day. To supply some comforts, three camp directors coordinated campfire activities. During evening hours when other Congress participants slept, the eco-camp crew in the wilderness had jam sessions. Performers, both local and part of the Congress, brought their musical instruments and joined the chorus of voices. From the Beatles to Jewish folk songs, the melodies connected villagers each night and stole hours of sleep. Carefully selected vegetarian meals with mostly organic and local produce provided nourishment, while the group enjoyed games and sports that promoted peace—canoe paddling and surfing. Hawaiian culture, hula, and language lessons enhanced the experience and introduced us to the indigenous inhabitants and ways of these islands. Most even became "hanai," or adopted family; shared many "pules," or prayers; exchanged "ha," or breath; and accepted Hawaiian names.

Overall, the eco-village won major applause from community members, lawmakes, and the press who explored the environmentally conscious and portable village. At the close of the Congress, the structures were returned to the University of Hawaii Manoa campus to be displayed and later donated to a summer camp.

Erin Mendelson

Malama is the Hawaiian word for caring but with a deeper sense of treasuring, cherishing, caressing; **Malama a'ina** - means caring for the earth - the environment, but with that deeper sense of treasuring and caressing every thread of life within its fabric.

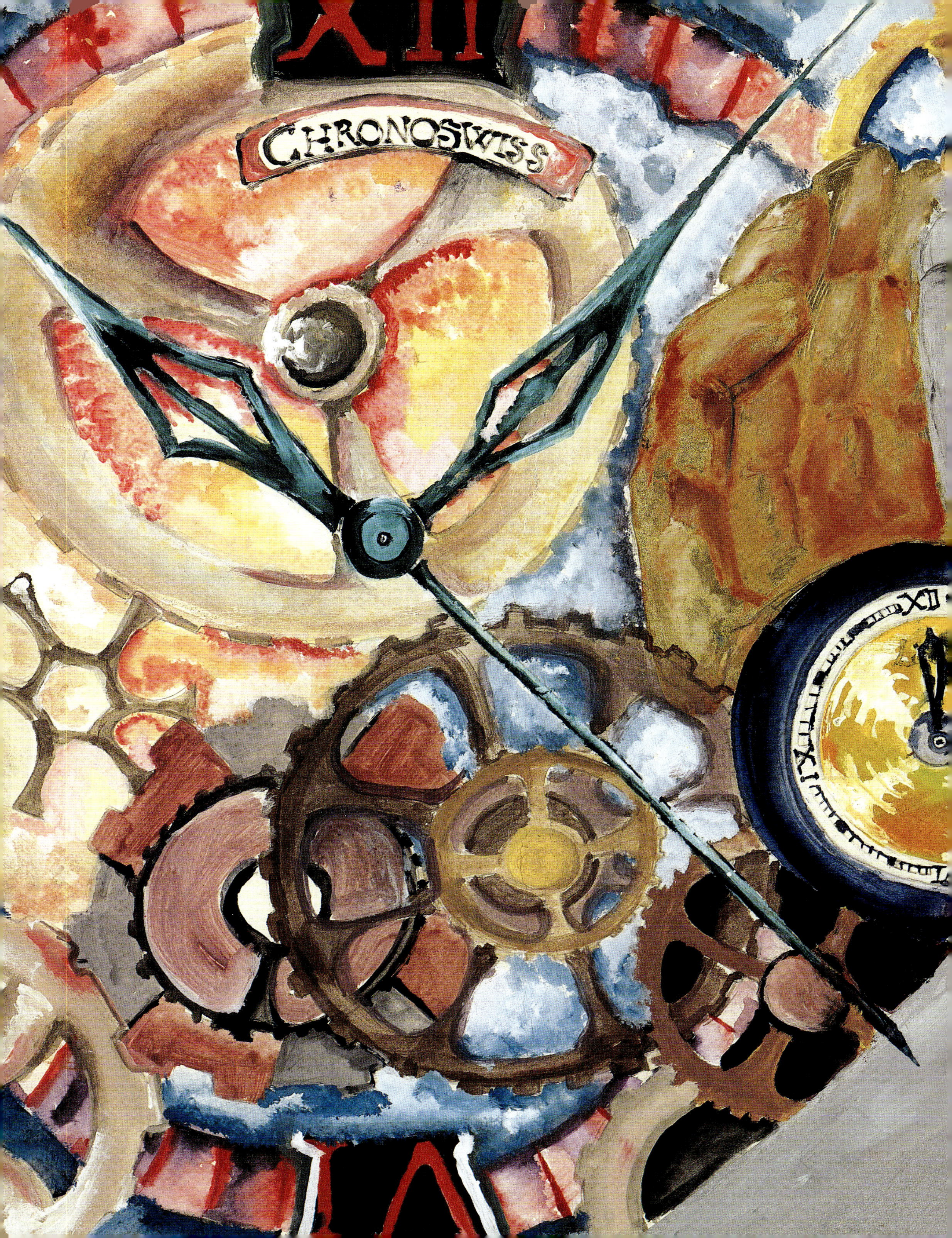
CHRONOSWISS

Priorities & Actions

- Education
- Peace
- Environment
- Human Rights
- Health
- Poverty
- Population
- Corruption
- Economy
- Democracy
- Animal Rights
- Substance Abuse

Priorities

Education
education, Education...

> (Education is a light in the darkness and a hope for the world.)
>
> Ghanaian delegate

Extraordinary, isn't it, that young people around the world all agree that education is the top priority for the world in the new millennium! Why did we? Because we believe that, if every young person is educated and encouraged to work toward environmental protection, human rights, democracy, health, sustainable development, tolerance, and fairness, all the other problems will vanish over time.

What young people need is a good listening to!

When young people are given responsibility, generally we behave responsibly. If we are denied responsibility, who can blame us if we are irresponsible! In most schools, **NOBODY** even listens to us! We are herded like cattle into cages where teachers treat us like little kids. They cram facts into us and expect us to repeat them at examinations marked by them. Where is our input? Governments have promised again and again, at the Rio Earth Summit and countless UN conferences, that young people would have a voice in matters that affect their future. Why don't they start with schools? A good place of learning is one where teachers and the taught all feel part of a cooperative learning experience. Some schools have youth councils, but often they only discuss cafeteria meals and school parties. We need youth involvement in planning the curriculum—and the selection of teachers. Some schools welcome kids into the governance process—and they are some of the most successful schools on the planet. But mostly, youth are ordered to just obey the rules. Governments must legislate to allow us help govern our schools.

Education for all

We are disgusted by the stories we heard at this Congress of schools so poor there is no furniture, no windows, and no paper or pencils. When world leaders came together in Jomtien, Thailand in March 1990, they promised "education for all by the year 2000!" Here we are, days away from that date, and there seems no sense of urgency to achieve that goal. Why doesn't anyone ask us to help? There are 13-year-old girls in Pakistan running schools, giving basic education to other girls. In Nicaragua, teams of young people helped to raise the literacy rate from less than 30% to over 70% in two years. How can our friends in developing countries take part in the great internet boom if they can't even write their own names? Education for all is a must for our future. Governments must harness our energy and skills to achieve it.

Education for life

As well as learning math and history, the urgent need for our generation is to learn how to live sustainably with our environment. We need to learn about peace, conflict resolution, and population growth, what good health is and how to achieve it, what our rights are and how to protect them ... all the challenges that we discussed at this Congress which really affect our lives—more so at least than Latin or trigonometry! Until schools teach us these vital-to-life issues, young people will feel increasingly that schools are irrelevant and that the real education happens outside and on the Internet.

The editors interpreted this untitled piece differently. Some see it as kids getting drawn into an intellectual vacuum where they are processed to repeat the mistakes of the generation before. Others see it as a positive vision of young people drawn out of the shadows of ignorance through a rainbow-brilliant school of the future that sets their minds on fire with understanding of how to live in harmony with each other and nature. What does it say to you? Think of a title for the painting!

untitled, by Yana, Estonia

Priorities

Education around the World

Europe

When the European region delegates discussed education, a major theme was the type of education that we receive. We need much more practical and vocational education. Why do we need abstruse math formulas if we aren't taught how to eat healthfully? Many believe that education for sustainable development should be taught as a subject—a curriculum based on how to live your life without harming the world for tomorrow's generation. The global priorities agreed upon at this Congress are a great place to start. They are all extremely complex and deserve substantial periods of school time and good teachers to explore them. Young people need to be involved in curriculum forming. We know what we need to learn: we deserve a chance to ask to be taught those things.

Less exam-based learning is also important. If exams are needed, there should be less pressure on students to achieve well: we were shocked by stories from Japan and Korea where students are encouraged to work 20-hour days to make top grades in exams. There has to be more to life than exams! It is not so bad in Europe because there are many opportunities for higher education. But in India and parts of Africa, the shortage of places in higher education means parents and teachers put intense pressure on students. This can be very negative and can lead to breakdowns and sometimes suicide.

(Education is a continuous acquisition of knowledge, from childhood until time of death.)
Anonymous

EDUCATION AND TRAINING

Africa

Unfortunately, for most Africans, going to school is a dream that will never come true. People are expected to live productive lives without knowing how to read and write. Many African countries do not have the facilities to educate the whole population. They are investing money in short-term projects rather than long-term ones that will result in future economic gain for the country. This short-sightedness is causing massive violations of what should be a basic human right to education. Money should be put into education; with education comes rapid economical progress. As well as this, there is the old mentality that girls should stay at home and work; however, there are signs that this conventional thinking is beginning to change. For those who are lucky enough to enjoy the privilege of starting school comes another obstacle. Often, there is a high drop-out rate because parents cannot afford uniforms or transport and they need the children at home to work. Another huge problem exists in scattered rural settlements. Often there are not enough resources to equip schools properly. Many schools are set up, but they fail to provide an adequate education because they do not have enough books or furniture. Teachers end up being disheartened and uninspired. Who can blame them? It is an endless battle to get materials that are up-to-date and interesting. There is also corruption within many systems which leaves many talented teachers without pay for months. No wonder they leave teaching, abandoning many talented and hard-working young people without a place to study.

Within African schools, there are other major flaws. Schools tend to be very backward: learning is done "parrot-fashion" and so many young people never learn how to think for themselves. Practical subjects such as woodwork and farming are not ordinarily offered, and so no vocational basics are acquired before stepping out into the job-seeking world. Listening to the cricisms of other youth at this Congress I was amazed. African youth are scared to criticize their school systems. They get a bad reputation as rebel and trouble-maker. Often parents discourage any radical action, but in Africa we urgently need radical action. We are a developing continent. We need to think about what our continent needs and dump the old European models of education. It is as if Africans feel they need to compete with Europeans, whereas we know we need to set our own educational standards and provisions to meet the needs of our continent in the next century.

Priorities

Education for All (?)

(Women need to be educated. There are no buts, ifs, or wherefores. It is a fact. Women have a right to education. Everybody has a right to education, no matter what gender, color, tradition, culture, or religion. It is immoral and wrong to prevent anybody from getting an education in their mother tongue. Everything has to be done NOW to get ALL people a GOOD FREE EDUCATION!)

In our first book, we quoted an official from the World Bank who said that giving a girl a basic education in a developing country cost about $30—"and it is the best $30 you ever spent!" Since then, we have seen the Grameen Bank grow out of Bangladesh around the world providing women with small loans to start up businesses. And—surprise, surprise—women are far more reliable about making their repayments than many men. All over Europe, league tables have shown girls doing progressively better than boys in exams in every subject. Women are breaking through "glass ceilings" to leadership positions in all fields. In Peace Child itself, men are a minority in many of our most radical programs. Many of the best national coordinators are young women.

It is a complete scandal that in some countries women are prevented from going to school—prevented from getting their feet on the first rung of the ladder leading to responsible positions in society. Economies are the major losers in this as women are the driving force behind so much new thinking, growth, and prosperity. And it is a fact that educated women have fewer babies, thus helping to solve the population growth issue.

The age-old debate

Father: Why do you want to go to school? Education is for boys but you are a girl.

Daughter: Through the means of a good education, I want to shape and brighten my future! Is there a difference in aptitude between me and my brothers? I also want to become an officer or doctor as they shall become.

Priorities

Are There Schools in Our Future?

> Education is the window through which we can see the world.
>
> Raolu Thapa, 17, Nepal

The short answer is, "YES! Of course!" There is no better place to learn to read, write, become numerate, study books, and learn teamwork etc., than within the four walls of a school. But "education" comes from the Latin "e-duco," to lead out—and we firmly believe that a good education will lead us out of the schoolroom into the real world, with masses of practical projects and service work in the community. We are impressed by the story of a school in Fiji that converts waste from breweries into fish food; saving the community from vast mountains of waste and making money from the sales to support poor students to come to the school.

Schools should encourage more youth-led sustainable enterprises of this kind. We are also impressed that schools and colleges, by their nature competitive and stressful, are turning out "planetary vandals" not "planetary carers."

There are strong arguments for "de-schooling" society, but we think that schools should survive as long as they become committed to teaching sustainability and participation and adjust so that every aspect of their work is in harmony with their natural and community environment.

The Right to Illiteracy

Asuquo bassey Asuquo, Nigeria

Education for every Nigerian Child?
A mirage-because it is expensive
Because my parents are poor
Because books are expensive
Because we children work for money
Some hawk in the streets
Some care for babies
Some have children of their own
Illiteracy is your right my child,
Education is for royalty
Education is only for the rich
Education is foreign to us all!
We are twelve in the family,
Only two can go to school
But we have no hope for school
Because admission is hard
Because education is done by quota
Because some states are educationally advantaged,
Because some states are disadvantaged;
Give all children the right to school ! Yes.
But because schools are few
Because teachers are few
Illiteracy is here to stay!
Illiteracy is our right—our way of life!

Case Study:

In the UK, PYPA 21 (Plymouth Young People's Agenda 21) is just the kind of out-of-school environment that we should have more of in the future. Run by a youth committee with adults on the City Council, it pursues a locally-based action agenda of environmental conservation and improvement, craft development, social action, book writing, and Agenda 21 promotion.

Our group has inspired similar groups in Peru—in Lima (LYPA 21) and Cusco (CYPA 21). We now have links with these groups and are discussing cooperative projects while learning at first hand from kids of our own age the realities of life in the developing world.

Education for sustainability cannot just be done in a classroom: it has to get kids out into the real world—north and south—to experience what needs to be done.

(Peace, love, and education are the foundations of a happy life. Without understanding, you are able to accomplish nothing at all. We all need to be educated in love and peace. Consider this and put it into practice. Better your surroundings by bettering yourself.)

Sam's words, ELCIN Nkurenkuru High School

"My life is miserable"

That morning I woke up very late. I grabbed my breakfast and backpack. I ran to the bus stop in a vain attempt to reach the bus, but to my surprise all my friends were still waiting for the bus. It was delayed by twenty minutes. Minutes later we went to school in my dad's car. When I arrived there was a wrecking ball crane trying to knock our school down. We asked a man who was in charge of the demolition, why were they doing that? He said, "This is a matter of the government."
We found out later that the government had cut off the budget for public education because the international financial funds demanded that our country pay its foreign debt as soon as possible. Therefore, all the public schools had to be closed down.
 I was thirteen years old. My friends went to private schools because their parents could afford them. My parents couldn't. So I stayed at home like a layabout. When there was nothing to do, I went into the street and found new friends. That was the beginning of the end.
The following year I started stealing. In the beginning, it was little thing's, jackets, handbags, until I decided to start using guns for my robberies.
It didn't help much; I was caught by the police and put into prison. My parents thought I was a lost cause and chose not to be involved. I started taking drugs when I was in prison. After six months I was let out. Nobody was there to give a hand, guide me or support me, so I found relief in alcohol.
Now I am thirty-six years old, and I live under a bridge. I depend on a woman who gives me vegetables to eat. Who is responsible for this? I wonder.

Lying down under the stars, when I dream, I dream about a new nation, with accessible and free education for every child, where values that have never been taught to me, such as love, friendship, honesty, and loyalty, are taught.

Pancho, Ecuador

Priorities

Time for Action!

Congress participants matched their commitment to education as top priority by making more action plans on the topic than for any other.

Computer Plans

Computers are rapidly changing. You buy one on Tuesday and by Thursday a new, better model has been launched. For schools, especially in undeveloped nations, to come up with the money to buy these expensive machines can't always be possible.

In the Cook Islands a group called Computer Kidz applied to the Millennium Action Fund to buy three new computers. They need to keep ahead in technology to have a better chance of getting employed in a difficult job market.

In the UK the government runs a scheme which lets colleges apply to be a technology college. They then receive extra money to buy equipment. A personal experience of technology colleges: "We are very lucky to be a technology college. Not only do students have access to digital cameras, new computers, the Internet, and scanners, we also have an excellent team of highly qualified computer technicians. What is the point of having a computer if you don't have someone to fix it and know how to operate it well?

"We also share the equipment with the local community. There are adult education classes in the evening, and we share the equipment with other local schools. Students are actively encouraged to use the computers, especially the Internet."

Thomas Burke, Eggbuckland Community College—A UK technology college

Mere words won't do. We must all take action. There were tons of action proposals about education, from educating expectant mothers in Morocco to improving literacy in Bhutan, with lessons in tolerance in Austria and pond renovations in the UK in between.

Pham Thi Thu Huong, the delegate from Vietnam, wants to go to remote villages in Vietnam and teach basic reading, writing, and math to those who are unable to go to school because they need to work to feed, clothe, and house their families.

ACTION Plan

Edu-Kids, a group in India, would like to eradicate illiteracy from their neighborhood. Each member will share knowledge with ten people who will share their knowledge with family and friends.

ACTION Plan

Pei Yin Tsai and Su Ju Tsai from Kaohsiung would like to work with the Sign Language Association to have a seminar teaching sign language to a group of students. They will learn signed songs, basic sign language, and a sense of the deaf culture.

ACTION Plan

I-POLY students and staff want to set up a project to promote their kind of education and develop a global citizenship curriculum. They propose to set up a hub from which students and staff can monitor efforts in global citizenship training, sending out teachers and students to advise and build curricula throughout the world. In this way, I-POLY hopes to raise the profile of global citizenship training and make it an essential component of every young person's education.

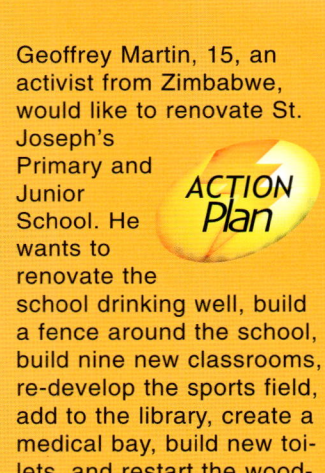

ACTION Plan

Geoffrey Martin, 15, an activist from Zimbabwe, would like to renovate St. Joseph's Primary and Junior School. He wants to renovate the school drinking well, build a fence around the school, build nine new classrooms, re-develop the sports field, add to the library, create a medical bay, build new toilets. and restart the woodwork and agriculture section of the curriculum.

ACTION Plan

Proposals submitted to the Millennium Action Fund, October 1999

by Aminu Seidu, Ghana

Priorities

Pace PAIX MNP PEACE

AMANI Frieden MALUHIO

By Tamsin Stroude, Uganda

Paz Shalom SHANTI Taika

Peace is the essential foundation for any kind of a happy life. How can we think of anything else if we do not feel safe? How can our lives be productive and meaningful if we are in constant fear of getting killed? Peace is the keystone on which we balance all other priorities. When war breaks out, all positive development stops and the destruction of life on our planet begins. During wartime, the primary aim of any man, woman, or child is to simply survive to see another sunrise. With vision and commitment, we believe our generation will achieve world peace. Only then will our other priorities be fully addressed.

Blackest Thursday...

I am lying on my bed, staring at the ceiling. My mind wanders back to Black Thursday when I was only seven years old. I woke up and switched on the TV to watch cartoons. I was surprised to see that Kuwaiti folk songs were being played. I went into the kitchen where I was greeted by dismal looks on my family's faces. They said nothing was wrong, and I pretended to believe them, but deep down inside I knew something was terribly wrong! My dad said, "She has to know." My knees buckled. I braced myself for the bad news. "Kuwait has been invaded by Iraq," he said. During the next six months, I would go through endless fear and anxiety. Looking through the window of my room, I saw and heard things that a seven-year-old girl should never have seen or heard.

One night that I will never forget, I was looking out my window and saw a jeep in our neighbor's driveway. The back doors opened and a blind-folded teenager was kicked out from the jeep. I recognized him as our neighbor, a boy who I heard had been taken a week before by the Iraqis. I was going to tell my parents when the Iraqis began knocking on the door of every house, including ours.

The teenage boy was guided by an Iraqi soldier to his house. His family was waiting for him at the doorstep, but he never made it inside. One of the Iraqis, still in the jeep, shot him in the head. I heard the thundering sound after the soldier pulled the trigger. I heard the loud thud as the boy hit the ground. I heard his scream before he fell. I heard the agonizing wail of the boy's mother. I heard the cold and inhumane laughter of the heartless soldiers as they were putting up a sign bearing terrifying words: "ANYONE WHO MOVES THIS BODY WILL SUFFER THE CONSEQUENCES." As they were driving off, I heard myself scream and cry and run to my mother. I remember the way she was trembling. I was not able to sleep without nightmares for many days later.

Lillian Gabra Fam, survivor of the Gulf War, Kuwait.

> We, the children of Bosnia and Herzegovina, hate wars. Wars make people so cruel and they don't care for learning and knowledge. So, please, STOP!
>
> "Saburina School," Sarajevo, Bosnia and Herzegovina

"You cannot understand how war has devastated my country these last ten years. Thousands died, including my brother, poisoning my heart with grief; buildings are shattered; all the shops are looted; the fields are peppered with mines everywhere you look. There are beggars sitting on carts, their feet and hands cut off by the terrorist rebels. It is terrible! Awful! How can there be any priority greater than peace—peace for all time, for all people, everywhere. Please, my generation, make it so!

Sheku Syl Kamara, Sierra Leone

Priorities

Poem for Bosnia

Everywhere I went they asked me:
Tell the world what's happening.
Tell what you have seen.

I will tell them, Aleksandra
How you spent twelve winter months
Crouched in the cellar
No warmth, no light, dead air;

How an entire high rise
Huddled in fear
Waiting for death
Counting each second hearing on the
Other side of the wall the bullets
Invading the tenderness
Of your homes;

And of how you took water
To those who couldn't move,
Risking your life
In the crossfire of the street,
One plastic bucket
In each determined hand,
And how it spilled
However hard you tried
To keep it steady.

Rosemary Mensies, Sarajevo, Bosnia and Herzegovina

Say no to nuclear!

Countries in my region are always threatening each other with nuclear weapons—but when did the people ever say they wanted to get involved in nuclear games? Innocent people are affected by nuclear weapons and war, and they don't even have a choice in the matter. Our leaders must respect each other and each other's people instead of thinking only about power and destruction using this terrible medium of nuclear weapons.

BuBuba Gurung, Jhapa, Nepal

17 seconds in the thoughts of a child in war

Today I hope for a crust of bread
my stomach is making funny noises
maybe it will scare off the troops
I almost forgot. Pembi is dead.
I will find a friend who can't die!

Monica Dias Dos Santos, Namibia

Case Study: On Cyprus

Europe's longest war still smolders on in this beautiful Mediterranean Island where an "Iron Curtain" known as "The Green Line" still divides the Greek and Turkish Cypriot communities. It has been so since 1974 when the Greeks attempted a coup to unify the island with Greece and the Turkish army then landed in Northern Cyprus. The Turks now occupy over a third of the island and have set up their own unrecognized independent state of North Cyprus. There has been a virtual political stalemate ever since. But, as demonstrated by the young Greek and Turkish Cypriot delegates at this Congress, it is perfectly possible for the people on both sides of the island to live in peace together, if the governments would just get out of the way and let them do it. Although meeting in person on the island is still almost impossible, the Internet is making it easier to chat and that is very helpful. The first thing everybody needs to do is to be able to truly listen to what others feel and want. Without that, there will never be peace!

Case Study: on Kashmir

This year, for the fifth time in the last 50 years, the sound of gunfire resounded in the beautiful mountain-state of Kashmir. Pakistan and India have fought over this territory since independence, neither willing to surrender hegemony to the other. Though divided, most Kashmiris would like to be independent, like their neighbor Nepal. But, as the majority of them are muslim, they would naturally ally with Pakistan against India. Because India's first prime minister, Pandit Nehru, was himself a Kashmiri, and because all Indians have a lot of love and money invested in Kashmir, they are not prepared to give it up. There is no resolution in sight, and with both India and Pakistan as proven nuclear powers, the situation is getting more and more dangerous.

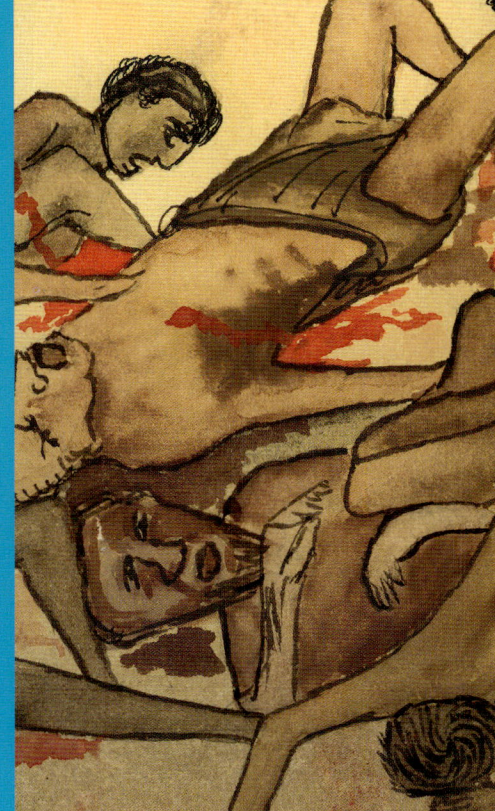

Case Study: on Northern Ireland

In 1998, the Good Friday agreement was hailed as the end of a 700-year dispute in Ireland between one group who had fought and died for a United Ireland and another that had fought and died for the union of Northern Ireland with the United Kingdom. With its all-Ireland institutions alongside its confirmation that Northern Ireland would always remain a part of the United Kingdom, the agreement contained many uneasy compromises and, perhaps inevitably, it has now started to unravel. The current problem is the speed with which the Irish Republican Army gets rid of its weapons. As we write, it is very hard to see a way out of the impasse. In both parts of Ireland, the people of Ireland voted heavily for peace. It is now up to their leaders to figure it out. But a decision that most kids would be able to take in a second seems to be beyond them! Pride, ego, and a ton of history weighs down on them, preventing them from doing what everyone thirsts for. Isn't there something we can do?

"During the past decade, wars have disabled and killed far more children than soldiers. About 2 million children have died in wars over the past decade; 4 to 5 million children have been maimed; more than 5 million forced into refugee camps and over 12 million left homeless," says the State of the World's Children 1995.

Priorities

His Holiness, the Dalai Lama, is one of the most extraordinary people alive. Though an exile from his country for most of his life, he seems to have found perfect inner peace and happiness. He brings joy and smiles to everyone he meets. He won the Nobel Prize for Peace, 1996.

"Let's build the house of Peace!"

If each of the priorities you discuss is a brick in the house of peace, isn't it time to abolish war? If we want to build that house, should we not also educate our children for peace?

Cora Weiss, President, Hague Appeal for Peace

Peace in the mind

Through industrialization, we hope to improve our standards of living and make our lives much easier. In the process of development, we have made ourselves restless, and the mind is no longer at peace. Life has become a burden because we have a lot to do and this involves countless hours of hard work. Tension exists in everyone's mind, and there is hardly any peace in leading such a busy life.

Dinesh M. Bhugayta, Kenya

International youth support on the web!

ACTION Plan

There is a need for a space where young people from all nations can communicate and share their perspectives of war. Having such a powerful tool like the World Wide Web, it is time to create a site to be in contact with those who are suffering and may need emotional support. Accompanying it, a newsletter will be printed and taken to the UN offices. An editorial team will provide the sustainability of the project.

Let the drums bring peace!

ACTION Plan

In Mürzzuschlag, a little town in green Austria, there is a high level of youth unemployment and a lack of skillful labor.
Over the last few years, aggressive conflicts have been growing among different youth cultural groups. Such an environment works against inspiration and motivation. As an outcome, the young people have left the town in search of more promising horizons. Many who remain lack culturally diverse understanding and communication skills.
Our solution to this problem is to motivate young people, give them the tools to spend their time more ingeniously, and develop "learning projects" at schools. These learning projects will include a series of percussion workshops called "Crash Boom Bang" which will be lead by a percussionist, an educator, and a psychologist. Aggressions will be worked off through drumming. A percussion theater-play will be performed at the end of the term for the general public.
The latter will be combined with "Lessons in Tolerance" where students will learn about other cultures and create a feeling of respect for other ways of living.
After a while, teachers and students will have the needed skills to deal with arising conflict situations and solve them before they grow bigger.

The Hague appeal for peace

ACTION Plan

In May 1999, 10,000 peace activists came together in The Hague to discuss how to make the new millennium 1,000 years of peace. They came up with a comprehensive action plan that, when implemented, could abolish war in our lifetimes, just as slavery and apartheid were abolished by previous generations. The main actions are:
• A global Campaign for Peace Education; for banning landmines and all small arms;
• A treaty to abolish all nuclear weapons;
• A Global Action Plan to Prevent War;
• Empower Young People.
YOUNG PEOPLE EVERYWHERE ARE URGED TO WORK FOR EVERY ASPECT OF THE APPEAL!

CONTACT: WWW.HAGUEAPPEAL.COM

Peace!

Everybody in the
world has a dream:
That the bell of
peace should ring.
That the end of war
should draw near,
And the streets
would be without
fear.
That we should not
fight over every little
mistake or demand,
Nor over a piece of land.
No more arguing, fight-
ing, murder or war,
Peace should reign for
evermore.
The kind of peace that is
more than a paper signed.
The kind of peace that would
remind,
That we are all flesh and blood,
That no matter what your faith
or race,
You are just like everybody else.
So, we of the new millennium
age,
Should prove that we can bring
the change,
End war and see the birth
Of peace for everyone on earth.
So if we want our world war-free,
Free of violence in the street,
A world with equality for all,
Everybody, big and small.
If we want this to come true,
We must all pull through,
We must complete the mission,
And bring to life our peaceful
vision.

Meital Rottstein, Israel

Priorities

Environment
Web of Life

If we imagine the earth's environment as a fragile spider's web, we can see each of its parts (plants, animals, human beings, air, water, and soil) as one among thousands of threads woven intricately together. We can immediately see how delicate the earth really is and how, by breaking just one of its many interconnected threads, human beings drastically disturb its natural balance. Right now, we are forcefully tugging the threads of the earth in different directions. Until we stop making war on our environment and regain a life in balance with nature, we will continue to edge closer and closer toward planetary disaster. It makes no difference whether you regard life as a fluke of circumstance or the creation of a higher power ... our environment, the life support system of ALL life on earth, must be treasured, not abused. And we all need to start acting now!

Oleg Zaharov, Russia

Once Upon a Time

Once upon a time,
rivers babbled
with life.
Now they are
choked with
rubbish.

Once upon a
time, forests
provided shady
homes.
Now trees look for
a home.

Once upon a time,
animals roamed the
plains freely.
Now houses and
factories line the
plains.

Once upon a time, fish
and corals flourished.
Now oil spills poison
the oceans.

Once upon a time, the
Earth was colorful, clean,
and vibrant.
Now the land is dry,
ravaged, and in pain.

Once upon a time, there was
more than enough space.
Now humans crowd that space.

Once upon a time, life on Earth
was in nature's hands.
Now life on Earth is in man's
hands.

Sheehan Lorenz, 15, Paraguay

Kristine Baubinaite, Lithuania

Priorities

Endangered Environment: What are we doing wrong?

The short answer to this question is "EVERYTHING!" But, as we learned from *Pachamama,* the UN Environment Program's new book by and for young people, launched at the Congress, we learn that a lot of good things are happening, but not nearly fast enough. Every individual in the world is part of the problem. Think about it.

If you come from a developed nation like Japan or the United States, you probably contribute to deforestation and global warming by consuming lots of paper, using the car a lot, and using lots of electricity by leaving lights on, etc. If you live in a developing country like Mali or Bhutan, you may have to walk miles each day to collect firewood for cooking, thereby sacrificing the opportunity to learn about environmental issues in school; or you use your nearby stream as a toilet or garbage dump, thereby contributing to water pollution. Bottom line: all of us contribute, beneficially or destructively, to our natural environment.

Threatened biodiversity

Brazil is a treasure house of animals, birds, insects, and plants. Half the species in the world live and grow here. Most are found in the Amazon Basin, where new species have yet to be discovered and named. However, because large areas of rainforest are being destroyed for grazing, farming, or mining, some species will become extinct before we have had a chance to even encounter them!

Donna Langton, England

City Pollution by Sasha Dzhevego, Ukraine

Experts say we are losing hundreds of plant, animal, and insect species every week, mostly because of deforestation. Cutting down rainforests also contributes to the greenhouse effect, because we eliminate greenery which converts carbon dioxide into oxygen. Also, many indigenous peoples depend on these complex ecosystems for their food, medicine, and livelihood. How would you like to see your home slashed and burned?

Life in the Sahara

Niger is a country that lacks abundant vegetation. The few trees that we do have are cut down by men to sell as firewood in the market, and after they have cut them, most do not replant trees. Happily, there is now a campaign to replant trees. The other big problem is rubbish. All the trash from Niamey is dumped in the countryside around the city causing all sorts of problems: wild animals come and eat the garbage, children cut themselves on buried trash and get sick from disease that gestates in the piles of rubbish.

Mireille Mignon, Congress delegate, Niger

Our planet's suffering is caused by
people
deforestation
pollution
loss of biodiversity
We recognize these problems but they
are always someone else's fault
"these problems don't concern us"
"I can't change the world by myself"

In the "developed" world we consume
many times more than
people in the developing world.
it is we who must change our habits
stop the extreme consumerism

Start with the little things
reduce—reuse—recycle
buy environmentally friendly products
take a bus or walk there instead of
driving
Stop whining and take action

Kaisa Niskanen, Finland

Priorities

Time for Action!

As you know, the goal of the MYPC was to give young people the chance to set priorities for the new millennium. As the Congress unfolded, this manifested in young people seeking, first, knowledge of the immensely grave challenges that await us in the next millennium, and second, the development of action plans which will enable us to BE THE CHANGE! We must be the motivation and inspiration to our peers, drawing support from networks of like-minded friends and mentors around the world. Take a look at some of these action plans: this is how Congress participants plan to save the planet, one small step at a time.

We are young and young people like to dream and it's perfectly alright to do so. But we must live up to our dreams and make them come true. We must act! So I am begging all young people just like me to join together and make these priorities we have established a reality. We do not have much time, my friends, and if we do not act quickly the new millennium will come and go. The question remains, however, if we will go with it! Stand up and say what you need to say, stand up and do what you need to do for yourself, for your fellow human beings, and for the planet.

Sharon Isaac,
Congress delegate,
Seychelles

(You have to be the change you want to see in the world.
Mahatma Gandhi)

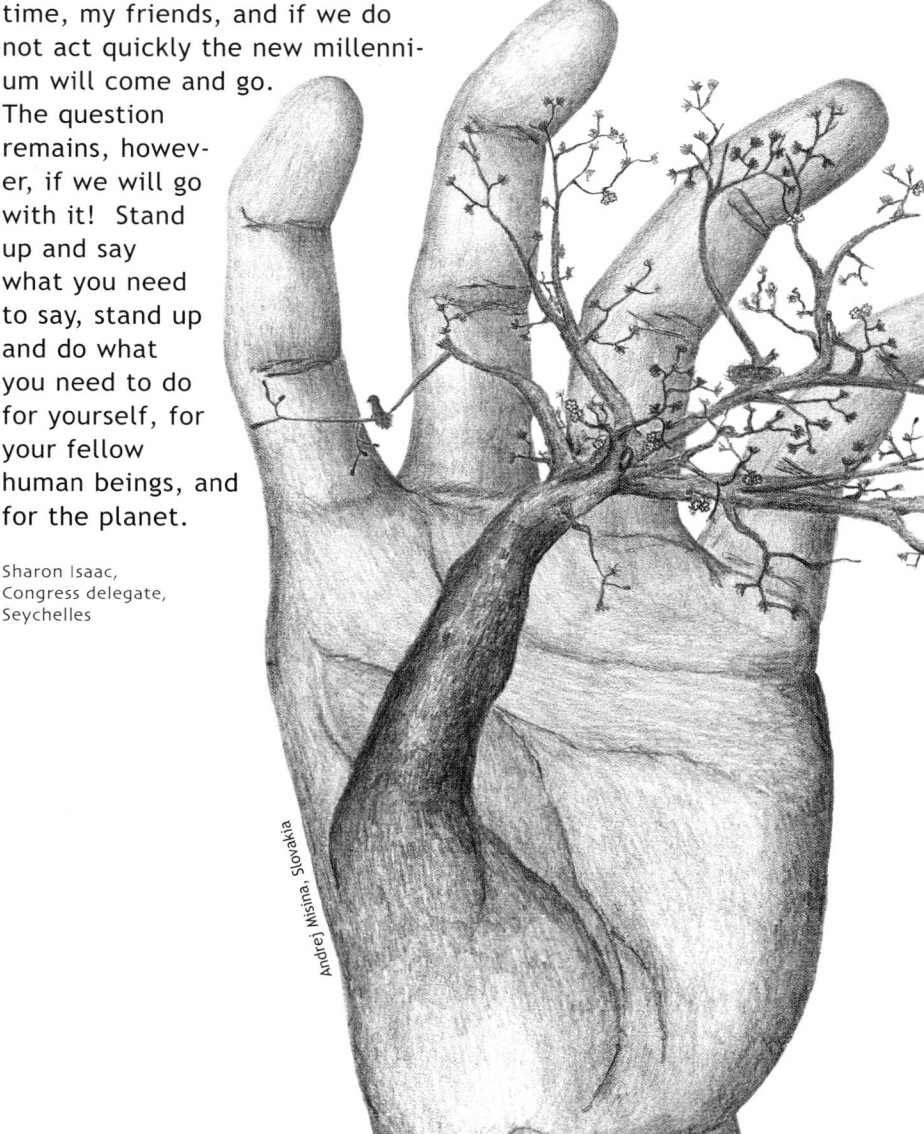

Andrej Misina, Slovakia

1. Using poop for energy

ACTION Plan

Problem: I am an 18-year-old girl who, all my life, has seen the destruction of the environment in my own country. This destruction, however, is not intentional. Through lack of education and poverty, the people of my country wastefully use firewood cut from our indigenous hardwood forests for cooking, lighting, and heat. Many animal species' habitats are being destroyed in this process of deforestation and soil erosion is already occurring where the trees once stood. Deforestation in Zimbabwe is also a problem. Soon there will be no more trees to use for fuel because they are not being replanted.

Solution: The people of my country need a different source of fuel for their daily needs. I propose to build a bio-gas plant at a cost of under US$2500 that uses human and animal waste to provide energy for a small village in place of firewood. When organic matter decomposes it gives off methane, an inflammable gas similar to natural gas used in households in the north. This will slow down the depletion of our forests and provide fertilizer for the villagers. Moreover, women and children will not have to carry firewood over long distances, enabling them to be more constructive with their time.

Shana Watermeyer, Congress activist, Zimbabwe

2. Waste to wealth

ACTION Plan

Problem: In our school community there is rampant wastage of paper. School projects and creative work require the use of lots and lots of paper. In India, one of the primary reasons for rapid and reckless deforestation is our burgeoning paper demand and consumption.

Solution: We plan to set up a mini-recycling plant in our school. We shall collect all waste-paper from each class and our neighborhood and recycle it. We shall make all varieties of unique recycled paper and sell it at a subsidized rate to school children. We already have a partnership with a commercial recycling plant, but transport of the waste materials costs a lot of time and money. If we had a mini plant at our school, the program would be much more effective and efficient. It would cost approximately US$2525, and we have received an enthusiastic response to this plan! We feel that if every student endeavors to make a conscious effort to use paper judiciously and recycle wastepaper, we are sure that diminution of deforestation will occur.

Dhruv M. Vasundhara, The Nature Club, Springdales School, India.

Larry Issa, Qatar

Priorities

3. 100 easy things I can do to save the planet

Action Proposal

Problem: I am a 17-year-old girl who is trying to do something to help save the planet. I think that we all must be aware of the danger we are in: the earth is dying and we will go with it unless we change the way we live. People need to be informed of the impact that each and every one of their actions, however small, has on the environment. I think it is important to think globally and act locally ... more people need to know this simple fact in order for the planet to stay alive.

Solution: I plan to design and distribute a pamphlet called "100 Easy Things I Can Do to Save the Planet." The pieces of advice will be practical but effective: turning off the tap when you brush your teeth will preserve our fresh water supply; riding a bike instead of driving a car will give you exercise and help to reduce air pollution. I will get help in writing the pamphlet from friends and teachers. The idea is that people who receive the pamphlet will photocopy it and hand out additional copies. This way, more and more people will learn.

Mariana Musi Cao-Romero, Congress delegate, Mexico

4. More bins, please!

Action Proposal

Problem: In my high school the problem of recycling and garbage is a growing concern. The ratio of garbage cans to the amount of garbage produced is very low—low enough that much of the garbage ends up on the ground. Moreover, the recycling system is almost non-existent. I feel that these two areas need drastic improvement to keep the school environment healthy and to heighten awareness of the students and teachers of what they should be doing with their waste. Education, though valuable, only costs time.

Solution: The first step will be for me to approach the student council at our school to address the issue. I will propose that there should be more garbage cans spread throughout the school and the surrounding areas. Our recycling program presently consists of three recycling bins that are located in the areas of heavy consumption at our school. They only cover the recycling of aluminum. I would propose that there be more cans with the capability of handling more types of recyclable products in more conspicuous locations. We plan to raise the money for the ten or so bins ourselves (through various fun fund-raising events such as dances, art sales, maybe even an auction of used goods) and to look after them."

Matthew Clarke, Congress activist, Canada

5. Wet and wild coastal clean-up

Action Proposal

Problem: We are members of a Scout troop in Dominica. Once a month we go to a different part of the island in order to clean up villages, tourist sites, parks, and marine sites (like a beach or an offshore reef). A while ago we noticed that some of the people in the poor community of Scotts Head were using the beach and the sea as a rubbish dump because the government had stopped collecting their trash on a regular basis. We contacted the local town council, and as a result better dumping facilities were soon provided. However, nothing was done about the already discarded rubbish in the ocean. Therefore, in order to protect the marine wildlife and the fragile coral reef ecosystem, we want to clean it up.

Solution: First, our troop will be certified in SCUBA diving. After this is achieved, we will undertake the underwater clean-up with the assistance of local professional divers. The villagers will pitch in and clean up along the coastline, and we hope to also teach them about the importance of not polluting the ocean because of its awful effects on the health of sea life and humans who live nearby. We also hope to involve the Wildlife and Fisheries Department in monitoring the area for any future signs of toxic contamination. The cost of this project is around US$1300, most of which we plan to raise ourselves. Once we are certified divers, we will be able to do this type of thing on a regular basis.

Marvin P. Marie, Congress delegate, Dominica

Soledad Bumbacher, Argentina

6. Recovery of an endangered species

Action Proposal

Problem: The biodiversity of our planet is increasingly threatened by human activity. The Holly tree, which is common in Galicia (Northern Spain) and other mountainous areas of Europe, provides many forest animals with an excellent source of food and shelter during the winter. The holly is also an integral part of the local forest ecosystem. However, because of its decorative value during the holiday season, the holly is ruthlessly cut down and is in danger of completely disappearing from the north of Spain.

Solution: We will devise an educational program to involve students in the conservation of the holly in our region. The program includes the construction of a greenhouse (which we will build ourselves), growing holly trees, and the reforestation of a protected mountainside area. We are a group of active students and have already worked on different environmental projects in our area such as the rehabilitation of our riverbanks, building of feeders for birds, the cleaning of our parks, planting trees and flowers, as well as posting signs to inform citizens of the need to look after our environment. We need about US$4300 to make this project work, but are confident that we will somehow get it!

Melina Barrio Martinez, Congress Delegate, Spain

> One person can help protect the environment, two can do even more. As you inspire friends and family, they'll inspire others. So share what you have learned and watch the impact grow! It all begins with you and me.
>
> Phan Thi Thu Huong, Viet Nam

Priorities

✋Human Rights

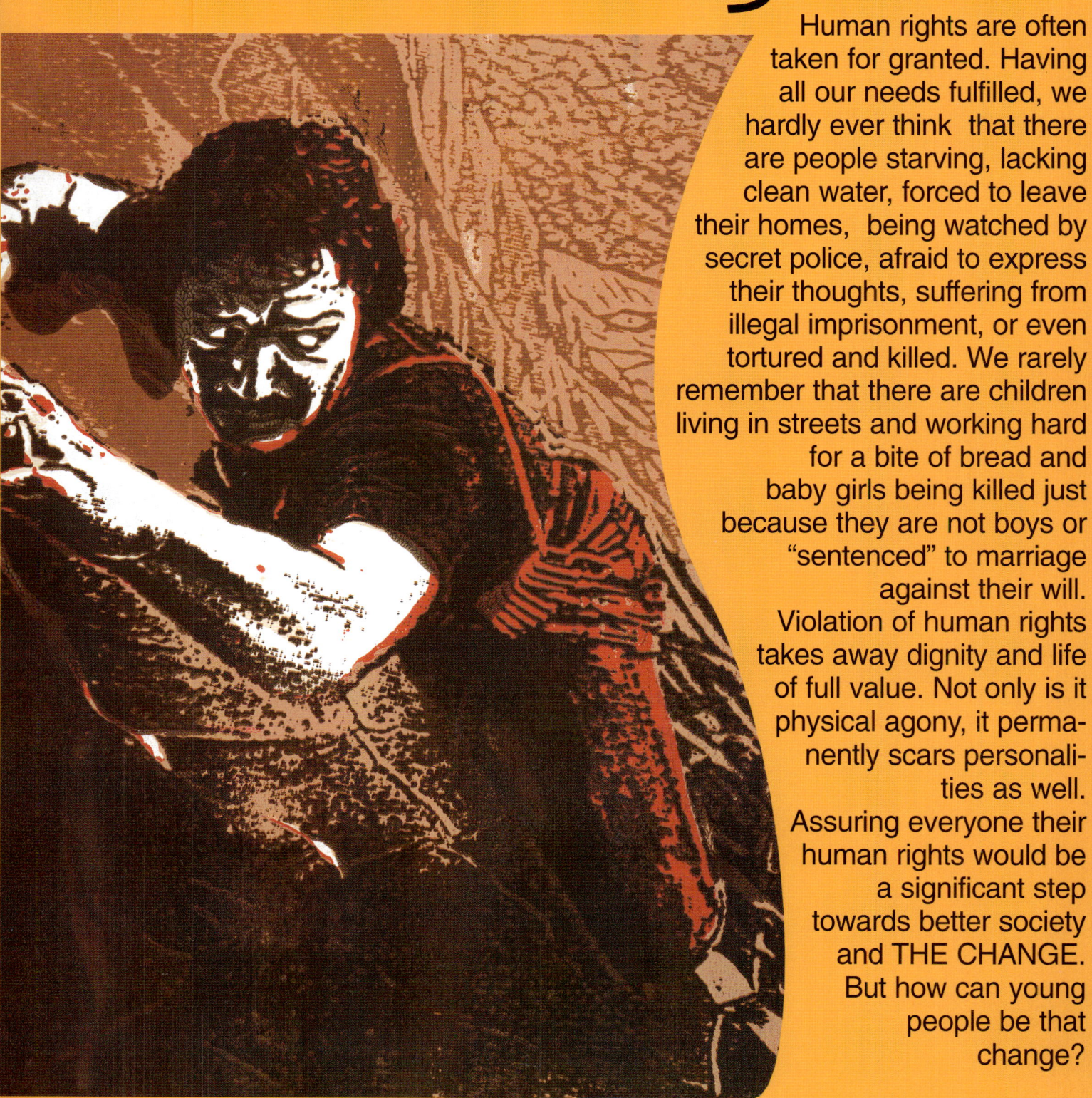

Human rights are often taken for granted. Having all our needs fulfilled, we hardly ever think that there are people starving, lacking clean water, forced to leave their homes, being watched by secret police, afraid to express their thoughts, suffering from illegal imprisonment, or even tortured and killed. We rarely remember that there are children living in streets and working hard for a bite of bread and baby girls being killed just because they are not boys or "sentenced" to marriage against their will. Violation of human rights takes away dignity and life of full value. Not only is it physical agony, it permanently scars personalities as well. Assuring everyone their human rights would be a significant step towards better society and THE CHANGE. But how can young people be that change?

Artist unknown

Artist unknown, Zambia

(You never know what human rights are taken away from you. By then is too late.)

The Nigerian prison

A place of punishment
Hell on Earth
A place of torture, grief and pain
Dark-hot, stinky-cold;
A place of misery and regrets
Separated from friends and foes
Some die before their trial begins
Some die of hunger,
Some of sickness
Some read the scriptures, sing and pray
Some learn a vocation, some a trade
But some transform from bad to worse
All in a Nigerian prison.

Asuquo B. Asuquo, Nigeria

FREEDOM!!

Freedom to raise a voice against ill treatment is the first and foremost right that enables individuals to expose their inner talents. Bhutan is just one example where a state has oppressed its people so far that now 100,000 are living as refugees in neighboring Nepal and India. Better freedom as a refugee than a silent, oppressed citizen.

Human rights are only a dream for Tibetans, who survived Ethnical cleansing.

Don't call me

I wish that ...
At school,
I wasn't called that black boy,
My shoes weren't hidden,
And my lunch wasn't stolen.
I am not offended for the "black"
But I am for the "that"
Whose scorn I feel
And I can't understand.

One day I asked my mother
Why I couldn't be handsome
As the other boys
Why I had bug eyes
Why my lips were big and thick

And she said ...
That's destiny,
And she seemed resigned
But I saw a tear
Coming down from her soul.

I only wish that ...
At school
I wasn't called "that" black boy.

Rosa A. Grijalva V., Ecuador

Action Plan

PROBLEM
Most Koreans don't know about Tibet. There is no student organisation related to the free Tibet movement even though Tibet is almost a neighbour and is one of the biggest Human Rights issues in the world.

SOLUTION
We, students at Korea University, will register Students for Free Tibet Korea. It will mobilise awareness and campaigns in Korea to support the Free Tibet movement worldwide.

Tibet

Tibet is a land of Buddhism, yak-butter tea, deeply religious and peaceful people. Because of the peacefulness of Tibetans, the Chinese army easily occupied this "roof of the world" 50 years ago. Since then human rights have been only a dream for the remaining Tibetan people who survived the ethnic cleaning —the cruel slaughter, torture, imprisonment, and forced sterilization of Tibetan women. Further, the Chinese have worked to erase Tibetan culture and religion by destroying Buddhist monasteries and other cultural heritage sites.

Chinese authorities are afraid of a massive revolution, so they closely monitor the lives of Tibetans. Foreign tourists have great difficulty entering Tibet, especially if they are members of any free Tibet movement. His Holiness the Dalai Lama has been a great leader for Tibet, but in exile. The situation has not improved yet because governments do not wish to jeopardize their trade with the buoyant Chinese economy. Money talks: culture and human rights have no credit rating!

Jelka Fric, Slovenia 18

Priorities

THOSE, WHO CAN'T PROTECT THEMSELVES

The lonely child sat on the ground,
Glancing casually, but I saw fear in those eyes.
A child so small
Yet so brave
To live a life
On the streets.
A life so dirty and discrete
How can someone just walk by,
Leaving a helpless child there to die.
Well, I'm not so proud at what I did
For all the stares in the neighborhood,
I bent to my knees
Smiled and said
"Do you need a friend?"
He glanced at me, unsure of himself
And wept, wept, then fell into my arms.
I took him home
Fed and clothed
The stranger, young but old
That night
So long
That night,
So cold
That night
I promised but never told
My secret
I used to live like that child,
Alone and scared,
Terrified to the bone.
Then a stranger came along,
And did what I did,
Said what I said
And gave that child
a second chance.

Anonymous

A little baby

Lies quietly in the corner — abandoned
The little child is
Sad—
Frightened—
Lonely—
Fragile—
The picture of innocence.

A little baby,
Breathes in its first breath.
It breathes in the odor of
Blood—
Pollution—
Poverty—
Death—
An intoxicating smell of the earth dying.

A little baby,
Listening for its first noise
It hears children crying for
Food—
Love—
Shelter—
Education—
And a happy life.

A little baby,
Crying for something to taste,
Weeping for its first meal,
Starving—
Famished—
Hungry—
Feed me please,
Don't starve me to death.

A little baby,
Taking its first look around,
It sees,
Children crying,
People dying—
Polluted waters—
Homeless, jobless people,
A world not meant to live in.

A little baby feels for someone to hold her,
There is no one there,
Don't leave me!
Don't abandon me!
Don't destroy me!
Don't kill me!
I'm your little child!

A little baby thinks,
What will the world be like
If we do not,
Get up!
Stand up!
And fight for HUMAN RIGHTS.

Bushra Razack 12, South Africa

Look Inside

We
may not have the
same color skin
You may not wear the same clothes
I'm in
We may not walk and talk the same way,
We may not go to the same church on Sunday,
We may not hold the very same rank,
We may not have the same money in the bank
It's what's inside of you and me
That is more important than what you see
So if you want to look inside
I'll guarantee
The only thing you'll find is my personality.

Stephanie MacDonald, Canada

The tale of a little Indian child

A twelve-year-old boy's father died in a car accident two years ago. Since then the entire load of supporting his mother, sister, and six-year-old brother has fallen on his young shoulders. He works in a plastic recycling plant. Little does he know that this is an illegal establishment. It does not follow any safety norms. The workers are constantly exposed to poisonous fumes that are hazardous to their health. For the past month he has been suffering from acute breathing problems. If anything were to happen to him, what would become of his family? They would beg, get sick, go into prostitution. and die young.

There are hundreds of such boys all over India suffering under similar conditions, their health under constant threat from dangerous chemicals, with extreme low wages. They have no savings to fall back upon if they lose their ability to work. The need to provide income for their family has completely deprived them of their childhood.

Depriving a child of his childhood is actually more barbaric than killing him, for if you deprive a child of his childhood you give to the nation an uneducated, gullible, simple-minded, permanently poor citizen who will always be a burden to society.

Juhi Nagarkatti, Indian Delegate

The child in Africa

The child in Africa
Thin, bony and yawning
The child in Africa
Running and crying
The child in Africa
Running and falling
War is in the continent

The child in Africa
Naked in the street
He runs and sings his sorrowful song
As he sees his parents fall prey to the guns

The child in Africa
Running away from fat flies
And licking his nostrils with his tongue
Biting nothing but his own teeth
Swallowing nothing more than his own saliva

The child in Africa
Caught in the trap by hunger
He lives with no food to eat! Oh starvation
Parents fight but he suffers

The child in Africa
Guarding his dead mother and father

Tears running down his eyes
As he feels his parents cold like ice

The child in Africa
Lying by his parents with nothing to drink
He looks on! Left and right
But no one to say child I love you
Misery! Oh misery, this pure misery
Living this world far from caring.

N. Daniel Juwel Ngungoh, Cameroon

Delphine Hesters, Belgium

PROBLEM:
There is an increasing number of children living on the streets of Brazilian cities: in the sidewalks, parking lots, parks, and bus terminals (during night time). Most of them are run-away children from nearby towns and provinces and some of them are abandoned and neglected. In the streets those vulnerable children are exposed to all sorts of hazards. They are usually victims of abuse by some adults. They tend to be influenced by hardcore street children who have been immersed in a lot of vices such as gambling, drugs, alcohol, etc. Without guidance and assistance, these children will certainly land a wayward kind of life without direction.

SOLUTION:
A temporary shelter for working and run-away children staffed by young people who can befriend the street children, give them a bed for the night, and protect them from all sorts of danger.

Action Proposal

Priorities

Women's rights violation

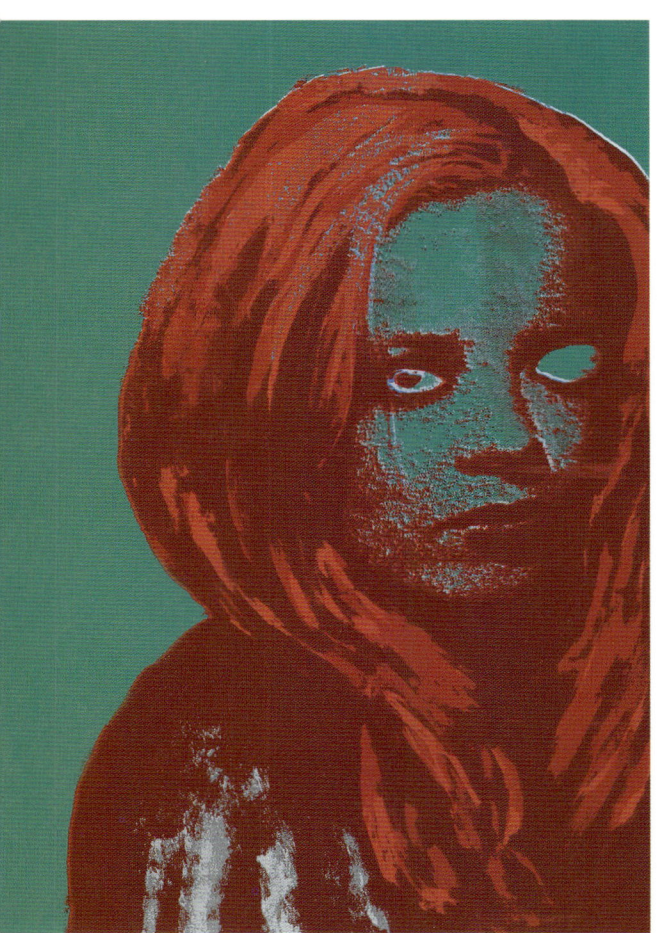

Gender issues did not feature highly in the Congress, but in the writing supporting the human rights priority, almost everyone recognized the horrific violations of women's rights that continue around the world. These writings are just a small sample of the cruelties heaped on young women around our world.

South African family

For many Africans, human rights do not exist. Through lack of education and illiteracy, they are unaware of their rights. "Family" established a hostel for homeless children to provide food, clothes, a place to live, and education.

Furthermore, they set up workshops where literate people teach illiterates to read, write, and understand basic environment and health issues. Homeless children and adults are given their basic human rights—to clean water, food, bed, and education.

Young prostitution

Each year thousands of young girls are abducted from Burma, Laos, the State of Yunan in China, and northeast Thailand.

There are girls that become prostitutes from duty. Parents expect their children to sell themselves for 25 dollars so the family can enjoy the comfort and the pride of owning a refrigerator or a color television set.

Most of the girls found as prostitutes didn't have a chance to get educated. They were fooled by the child agencies that promised them to give some work where they would earn more money than working on a farm.

Many of them catch diseases such as HIV from the customers but no one is really concerned by this. If they die young, as many do, there are plenty more where they came from.

Reflections

With a sideward glance, she looks at me
Her eyes, that childish smile, those rosy lips
Were mine yesterday.
Run away! Why does she not run away
To play with other children?
She reaches out to touch me
But all we touch is glass.
Her face changes—no longer young
No longer innocent but old and wise.

So he came with the night
And pulled her from her bed
Confused she cried—
But her youth was prematurely stolen
And her soul is crushed forever
He took her out of me
Now I am her—a night older
But a lifetime wiser with no more tears to cry
Because now life is cruel and men are unkind.

Anusha Jogi, Zimbabwe

Sentenced to marriage

The female newborn Macedonian Muslims of the village of Labunishte are betrothed while still in their diapers. This custom has been passed from great-grandfather to grandfather to match a female infant with a male child from another family. It is an indeed morbid scene to see the face of a girl smiling on a TV screen—at the age of few years only—while she is being congratulated for something she can hardly be aware of.

Many parents of such children are victims of the very same tradition. They have been part of it, they are aware of what evil they inflict on their daughters ... and yet nobody dares to break this tradition.

This is only made worse by the fact that these girls are allowed to finish their elementary education only. Afterwards they are forced to patiently wait at home until their "intended" completes his education and comes back to fetch them. The same tradition also considers it shameful for a girl to walk around the village alone. Girls are not allowed to communicate with anybody. They fear their parents, the parents of their intended spouse, and even the latter himself.

(Annually FGM causes over 700 deaths yet it remains a so-called "cultural tradition" in many countries.)

FEMALE GENITAL MUTILATION (FGM)

Mali is the second country after Sudan where Female Genital Mutilation is most widespread and still galloping and spreading at the speed of wind all over the country. The practice is not dictated by any religion; it is just a traditional consideration. FGM keeps women pure, reduces their sexual desire, and prevents women from sexual orgasms. FGM poses a serious risk; and the operation can be fatal.

During the '97 school holidays, in the village of Diagaba, FGM caused the death of 11 girls. Yearly, FGM claims 700 lives or more. So far no measure has been taken against the perpetrators. Since it is an act of assassination, it has to be banned and be considered an unlawful act.

Artist Unknown, Zambia

Duncan Richard, Tanzania

Priorities

✚Health (*Health is a state of complete physical, social, mental, and spiritual well-being; not just the mere absence of disease.*)
Dhruv Malhotra, India

"The Right to Life" is the first article of the Universal Declaration of Human Rights. Life to us means good health and a long life — and yet many governments spend more on military defense than health service for their citizens. Health services must be a top priority for governments to provide.

In discussions at the Congress, both health and education were considered an essential foundation for the development of any country. A healthy population creates a healthy society that encourages learning and teaches tolerance. A healthy workforce increases economic productivity. There are problems as well. A good health service needs a continuous supply of medicines, facilities, and trained doctors and nurses. In many places this is impossible due to lack of funding, lack of training facilities, and accessibility. Disease kills record numbers in many countries. Young people must mobilize to push for health education, training facilities, and more finance available to supply medicines and build health clinics.

Health Realities   Refugee's Present Health Challenges

Although we hear health conditions are improving, we do not see this. Hospitals have become careless and are ignoring patient needs. Medicine shortages are common. If you don't have money, you might as well go home to die. Hospitals and their kitchens are becoming so filthy that eating the food has become a health risk. Medical staff constantly complain about how they are underpaid. Many of them smuggle medicines out and sell them for extra income.

For some, this world is a paradise; for others, it is hell. We refugees are facing great difficulties. In our camps, we do not have any fresh vegetables or healthy food to maintain our bodies in health. Nor do we have the money to buy them if they were available. This has led to severe physical degradation and mental retardation. Only the most serious patients are seen in the makeshift clinics and even then they have to wait two to three hours before a doctor sees them. Often they just die waiting. Mortality rates are rising, and people are beginning to accept that a premature death is inevitable. Health staff are no longer working for the people but for themselves. The only hope for life is running water, and mercifully we have some of that nearby

Durga Acharya

Mr. Tata

Mr. Tata was 45, married with two children, living on a salary of $69 a month, working as a night watchman in the big town of Douala. Unfortunately for Mr. Tata, thieves broke into his company when he was on duty. His boss thought he was a member of the gang and threw him out of the job. The innocent Mr. Tata struggled in vain to get another job. In the course of his search, malarial fever struck him. He struggled to cure himself with his small savings, but the disease persisted. All his friends and relatives got tired of helping him.

So Mr. Tata sold all his things and rejoined his family in his village of Babessi, about 500 km from Douala. While there, he sold all his land so that he could go back to Douala to continue his treatment, leaving his family in the village. After about a month, Mr. Tata finished up his money because of the price of the drugs and because he had to bribe the medical personnel to get them.

After a couple of weeks, Mr. Tata could no longer pay his hospital bills and thus could no longer get any medical services. He was thrown out of the hospital ward, and he sat in the corner of a street asking for help from the people passing by. He had no means to send a message to his family, and after living in these appalling conditions for a few days, he died and was thrown into the mortuary.

Poor Mr. Tata! No health insurance in his country, no proper healthcare, corrupt medical personnel, and a careless government. Healthcare is a really sad problem here in Cameroon — and I am sure the situation is the same all over Africa.

Daniel Nguygoh, Cameroon

(**Man was created to enjoy excellent health, not to struggle with sickness and death.**)

Nazmeen Tamia Bhamjee, Malawi

Priorities

AIDS: A Millennium Killer

Far and away the most commonly raised topic by Congress delegates in the health area was AIDS — Acquired Immuno-Deficiency Syndrome. It has no cure and it has already killed 15 million. Forty million more are infected with the virus, which is the deadliest in human history. It is transmitted through sexual intercourse, blood transfusion, unsterilized injections and other surgical tools, and also from mother to unborn baby. AIDS alone means that some Africans can now expect to live only 40, not 60, years. And it is getting worse: with 16,000 new cases a day, it is going to get worse before it gets better. In rich countries, there are drugs that ease the pain, but they are not available to the poor. They just die, slowly and painfully.

Fadhili Waziri Kindamba, Tanzania

AIDS is a creator,
A creator of problems.
Poverty is at the center,
Then come orphans,
Poor economy, poor education.
It's a blight! Let's fight it!

Steve Muhola, Cameroon

AIDS makes life almost as bad for the surviving members of the family as for the victims. AIDS orphans living with their relatives are often abused or enslaved due to lack of resources. We must join hands to defeat it.

Olive Kabanga, Kenya

AIDS, what a terrible disease you are!
You sweep through the Universe like a bush fire,
You attack everyone,
Regardless of age and status.
Will we ever be free from you?

Khama E. Phiri,

Randolf Pinaya Perez, Bolivia

I have AIDS

I have always thought about what I would do if a friend had AIDS, but I have never imagined that I could have the disease. I have always tried to be informed about problems concerning me, but knowing, not believing did not help me. Everyday I think about my situation, my death. It's time to tell my parents; I can't go on hiding. I think, in the end, they understand. I feel self-pity for the things that I cannot explain. Everyone reacts differently. I have to tell my friends. They have always said that they would not reject anyone with AIDS, and they were right — they have helped me. They have done what my parents have not done — they have given me advice and thanks. They have made this death sentence lighter.

Aleix Mañosas, Patricia Meira, Sergio Pulpillo, Andorra

Mariana Baudino, Peru

(Every day 16,000 new people acquire HIV — 11 people a minute are sentenced to a slow and horrible death.)

Aids is a great killer

I feel awfully sad,
My hands are folded,
Tears of sorrow stream down my face,
A sorrow diffuses all over my body.
AIDS what have you done to people?

AIDS has taken my beloved people,
The smiles are no more,
The cheers are no more,
Well-known destroyer,
What a great killer?

Steve Muhola, Cameroon

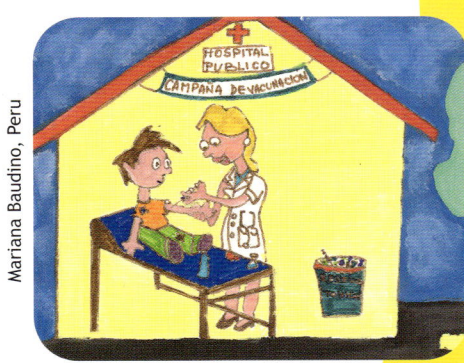

Vaccine Campaign Project

ACTION Plan

Sennur Delibas, a medical student from Turkey, feels child vaccination is very important. Many people don't have their children vaccinated because they cannot afford it or because they have to travel too far to get this done. He proposes to set up a mobile vaccination center with a nurse and two student doctors and go out to rural areas where families have no tradition of going to doctors or seeking medical help. He is asking MAF for the $225 start-up costs but hopes he will be able to raise it through local donations and contributions.

Immunization, Health, and AIDS Education Centers

ACTION Plan

Kuheli Bhattacharya and her group in India share a dream of health for all. She is concerned about the threat that AIDS poses to India in the new century as so few young people really know about it. She states that due to ignorance and long hours of low-paid work, the poor do not take their children for the free vaccines provided by the government. She wants to open up an immunization center and health education classes to alert poor young people to the dangers of AIDS. She plans to get started as soon as she gets home with the help of her mother and volunteer doctors.

Aids Awareness in Swaziland

ACTION Plan

Pascale Pavia also wants to alert young people in her country about AIDS. It is spread mainly by truck drivers traveling through. So she plans to erect 15 huge billboards, designed and built by her friends with the help of her father and a professional sign-writer, and place them at key points along the main highway. She has the permission of her government. All she needs is the money for the materials, and she has even got the paint donated.

Ladislav Soufek, Czech Republic

AIDS KILLS

Priorities

Poverty
Humanity's Shame

(There is something about poverty that smells like death. Dead leaves rotting around the feet like dreams falling to the ground.)

— Zohra Neal Hurston

According to the World Health Organization, poverty is "the world's deadliest disease and the biggest single underlying cause of death, disease, and suffering." This century has seen the building of welfare safety nets in many countries, but there is no global safety net. It is surely a priority task of our generation to build that safety net, and build it quickly before more people suffer and die.

Poverty Eradication

The eradication of poverty cannot be accomplished through handouts. Democratic participation and changes in economic structure are vital to ensure access for all to resources, opportunities and public services. Handouts creates dependency which is death to initiative and utterly destructive to the spirit of the receiver. However, in extreme circumstances, that is what people need to survive. So governments must provide social protection for those who cannot support themselves and to assist people afflicted by unforeseen catastrophe, whether caused by sickness, accident, natural or technological disaster.

— Twapasha Twea, Malawi

SLUMS

What is a slum? - a place with too many people crammed into houses that are all falling down; a place where rubbish and sewage mixes in the street and always smells; it is a place where people are all sick and all the children have runny noses. A slum is like a living sickness on the earth.

— Ssenyonjo Mark, Uganda

Artist unknown, Namibia

The Neglected
Right

When you buy something cheap
Do you wonder at the cost?
For the poor man starved and weak
And his children torn and lost

Do you think about the young girl
Toiling sixteen hours a day
To round your lovely pearl
And then still hungry, being sent away

When you see a 'posh' Designer name
Do you grin and buy it straight
Are you told of the people who have died or gone lame
Inside the miserable factory's gate

Life should be more than existence
These people need safety not pain
They need hope and a worthwhile future
To rebel from the Designers' game

Do you know of the working conditions
Or do you find them easier to ignore
Because you feel you can't change anything
Or perhaps you feel something more?

So if you have that 'feeling'
That you want to make things right
Think before you buy
And never give up freedom's fight!

- Victoria Holman

> No one who has not experienced the harsh reality of poverty can have a clue what it is really like: to try to sleep at night with your stomach screaming out for food; to be thirsty and know that the only water on offer tastes foul and is full of germs; to be achingly sick and have no doctor or medicines to turn to; to be confronted by an official with a form and not to be able to read the writing. To have no choices about where or how you live your life. Such is the reality of life for over one billion people in our world today. And it would cost only the interest on the wealth of the world's 40 richest people to give all of them a decent life.
>
> From the workbook prepared for the National Outreach process of the MPYC

(If we were to keep a minute of silence for every person who died in 1982 because of hunger, we would not be able to celebrate the coming of the 21st century because we would still have to remain silent.)

Fidel Castro, March 1983

Silver etchings from Ethiopia

Photo by Eco-Task Force, Patna, India

be the change

57

Priorities

nobody is going to give us a new world. We have to build it by ourselves and teach other people how to do it.

Marcos Ram Contreras Garzon, Bolivia

Artist unknown, Indonesia

POVERTY

What have we done to deserve this pain?
With sweat trickling down our faces
And tears in our eyes
We hold out our roughened hands
And cry out with bleeding hearts.
I ask myself why me? Why us?

Why can't I be like other children?
Why can't I also go to school?
And why can't I have a future?
Am I not worth it, am I different from what they are?
It's just that they are rich and I am poor.

Anina Ntia, Kenya

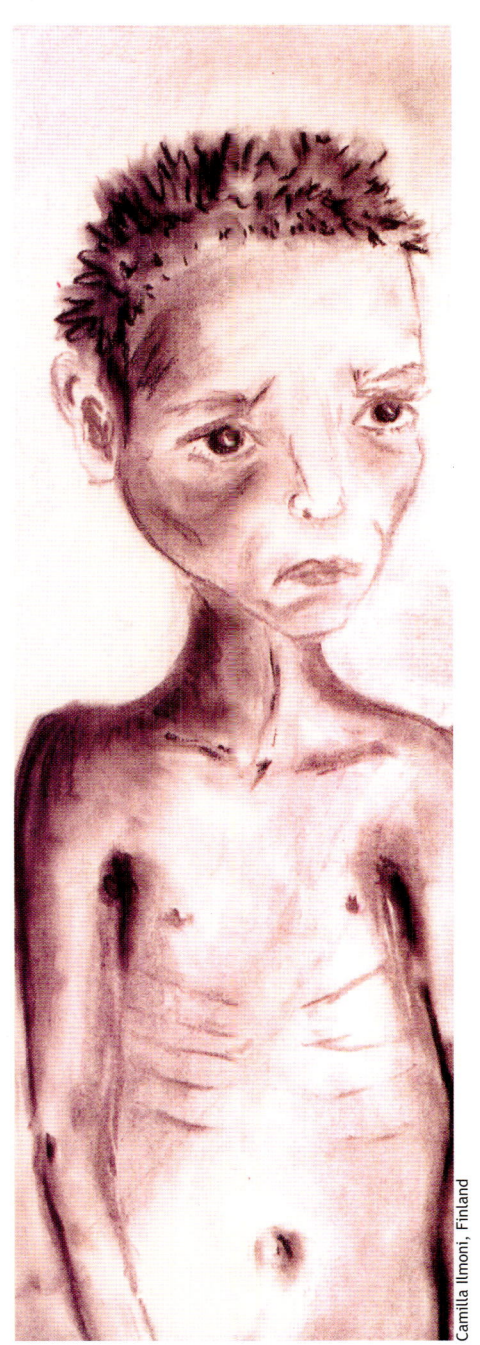

Artist Unknown, Qatar

Camilla Ilmoni, Finland

POVERTY

Poverty is a state of living in which people lack the basic necessities: food, water, shelter followed by love, safety, value, and purpose. The major causes of poverty are power and greed.

People need to change their power value system so that the more you share and care the more powerful you are. No one can change overnight, and it may be harder for some. If you start today with a random act of kindness it will make a difference.

If you haven't realized it already, we are destroying our world through greed. We need to educate people to realize this. Education gives you the power to understand and act upon things.

To me, "wealth" means having love for others before yourself. The statement "money can't buy everything" is true. Money equals material wealth. Love makes you have a sense of completion and happiness. This makes you truly wealthy.

Karen McKnight, Canada

Homeless in South Africa

Sitting in the cold on the side of the busy Eloff Street, watching the frost-bitten people walking briskly by.
Try and find warmth, somewhere out of this dreadful cold.
And all my worldly possessions are blowing away,
A cotton T-shirt and shorts is all I have to keep me warm.
A man, a tall rich man is coming towards me
Then before I know it he is kicking me
A policeman walks past and laughs at me.
I want to cry, I want to kick and punch but I could
Not because I am weak.
The last time I ate was two nights ago, it was like Heaven when I found that moldy, furry piece of
Bread in the dustbin behind that office block.
An old lady walked by, she looked like she could
Not even afford a loaf of bread,
But she dropped five cents into my outstretched hands.
It was the best gift someone could have given me.
South Africa can do with some more caring people
Like her. She was an Angel.

Dixon, South Africa

Doors unlocked— it's like paradise!

This is the first time I traveled out of Bolivia. Who would have thought that on my first trip I would come to Hawai'i? It's like being in paradise. My country is very poor. One of the things that impressed me the most was to see that, when I went out with my host family, we left the doors of the house unlocked. I wish we could do so in Bolivia. If we did that back home, when returning, we wouldn't find anything. Our house would be nothing but empty. There is such a high level of poverty that to satisfy their needs people break into houses and take as much as they can.

Randolf Pinaya Perez, Bolivia

Suraj Bhan, India

Mohammed Baker, Jordan

Priorities

Population
...How many more can the Earth support?

Days before we came to this Congress, the world population crossed the six billion threshold — up from one billion at the start of the century. It's now growing at a rate of 80–90 million a year, 9,000 an hour, 150 new babies each minute. Experts calculate that humans use 45% of the resources generated by the energy from the sun. Clearly, keeping our population within the Earth's capacity has to be a major challenge for our generation.

Since human beings live in communities, human couples— due to economical, feeding, and educational limitations— have had to be responsible for the control of family size. Otherwise, a couple who would have started having sexual relations at the age of 20 would have more than 20 children once the reproductive period of the woman had finished. Abortion and infanticide were the traditional methods that men used to curb the growth of their families. The development of family-planning techniques made available a wide range of contraceptive methods which are very effective. But only one-third of the world's population has awareness of the different methods of contraception. This is the reason why one in three pregnancies end up in abortion.

Some cultures consider a child as another mouth to feed; others see her/him as a new pair of hands to work, offering greater economical security to their parents. In addition to this, some governments defend their population policies, believing that the power and prestige of their nations is in direct relation with the number of inhabitants. Others, worried about the population crisis, develop campaigns to promote family planning. China, with the world's largest population, has taken extreme measures. Couples are only allowed to have one child. If there is a second, s/he will not have a right to a name, identity, education, and health care.
There are plenty of birth control options that we can choose from, and it is up to us to control our burgeoning numbers.

Roberto Matthias Diaz Luden, Ecuador

Jelka Fric, Slovenia

BALANCE

Presently, the good ship Mother Earth is burdened with too many people. If we keep increasing her load in the way we are now, one day we will tip the balance and she will capsize and sink, taking **Life on Earth** with her.

Prasugya Phukan, Jordan

Priorities

A new population model

> Population is a root cause of poverty. Children become an economic burden and liability if they are too many. This results in impoverishment of families.

Like a runaway train, the population explosion is out of control and, although there has been some slowing, we are still heading for the buffers at frightening speed. So the story of our generation has to be the search for a sustainable balance between population and the carrying capacity of our globe. Overpopulation is not about numbers: it is about the balance between the number of people in an area relative to the resources available to feed, clothe, and house them. Only if an area can sustain its inhabitants without rapidly depleting the natural resources, can it be defined as a stable region.

Dhruv Malhotra, India

Factors Causing the Increase of Population:

*The high level of illiteracy and the lack of awareness, which lessen the use of pregnancy contraception.
*Beliefs, principles, and traditional practices that encourage:
— Refusal of divorce;
— Pride in having a big family;
— Polygamy.
*Premature marriage.
*Using children as a workforce in agricultural activities, especially boys.

The Demographic Impact on Environment

Rapid development and intensive exploitation reduce the power of nature to reproduce.
Intensive land exploitation creates a desert-like environment.
Intensive agricultural activity during drought periods decreases the amount of minerals from land.

Aziz Makami, Morocco

A child cries, "We are too many!"

Every second of the day,
I hear the wails of four babies
Crying for food and survival
The baby laments
"O, I wish I were never born."

No mother caresses this
child with care,
It's one among many.
For him survival is a battle,
a struggle.
There is no food for him to
eat,
He goes with a bowl begging
on the street.

There are so many children
born
How many can we care for?
How many will we feed?

I walk along the streets
And find multitudes of kids made
homeless
By means of overcrowded, impoverished families.

Ministers and kings, do something!!
Help, control this massive growth.
If humans go on increasing
Will you have enough?
Who will support today?
Support tomorrow?

O! World, we are too many!
If it goes on like this
There shall be no life left, not any.

I plead to you friends around the world,
Have one child or two,
That should be quite enough!
Children are a blessing from god,
Don't make them a liability.
I beg to you, O world
Stop this population growth.

Leonard Michael, Namibia

Priorities

Population Solutions
Youth as leaders in the fight against population growth

The primary purpose of the Millennium Young People's Congress was to find sustainable solutions to the problems that plague the world today. The Congress worked out many innovative solutions to the problem of overpopulation. Education and awareness about birth control and family planning were unanimously agreed upon as the most efficient long-term solutions. Other solutions included an expanded reproductive health infrastructure, education, and empowerment of women, and incentives for small families.

These are some of the action plans that our concerned delegates and activists proposed to the Millennium Action Fund to address the population priority.

ACTION Plan

In her action proposal to control population growth, Sharon Isaac, the delegate from Seychelles wishes to seek help from parents, teachers, the Ministry of Health, as well as her peers to educate teenagers about the ill-effects of an overgrown population and the dangers of teenage pregnancy. She aims to do this through the various media such as distributing leaflets and journals, presenting street plays to educate the common people, and using radio, television, and newspapers to disseminate opinion about overpopulation.

ACTION Plan

Sicolelwe Hlatshwayo of Swaziland plans to work with the Ministry of Health and NGOs to carry out awareness campaigns. She will also volunteer to help doctors in various programs such as contraceptive distribution and fertility tests, as well as disseminate information about various birth control methods such as sterilization, vasectomy, loop, etc. She plans to ask capitalists in her country to donate to this cause.

Kemal Uysal of the Bursa Local Agenda 21 Youth and Environment Club, and an activist from Turkey, also hopes to establish a population control campaign. Working with the National Education Ministry, he plans to introduce sex education in primary schools. He plans to publicize the importance of decelerating population growth through seminars, television, radio, and the Internet.

ACTION Plan

be the change

Priorities

☹Corruption Eruption

Immorality. Dishonesty. Greed. These are words that you would probably not choose to associate with your country. However, corruption is a huge problem for most governments of the world, particularly in developing nations in Asia, Latin America, and Africa. In fact, it is often the primary reason why a country does NOT develop! — money raised to build schools or pay off foreign debt is pocketed by greedy politicians. This leads to poverty and a host of other nasty problems.

(Some people barely live hand to mouth, while others embezzle government money and keep getting richer.)

S. Asongwed, Cameroon

Corruption is particularly destructive when people value wealth over competence and integrity.

Cephas Amedume, Ghana

Governments are striving to develop their countries, but they still slip public funds into their private pockets. So the question arises about whether they are actually interested in developing their countries. It is believed that charity begins at home. If the government cannot stop these acts of corruption within their own establishment, how can they control it elsewhere in the nation? Governments must establish a transparent administration, so that citizens can see how the country's money is being used and have confidence in their government's integrity.

Germaine Nyati, Cameroon

be the change
65

Priorities

Randolph Pinaya Perez, Bolivia

(Corruption is like diabetes—it cannot be cured, but it can be controlled.)

Monica Nydkabi Mercy, Kenya

Corruption is everywhere in the world, but it is in Africa that it is causing untold damage and misery. My country, Sierra Leone, is going through excruciating turmoil as a result of it. From 1967 to 1996, corruption became so widespread that it became a way of life. Billions of Leons were embezzled by government employees. Developments that were paid for did not happen; government institutions for health, policing, and education broke down completely because of this chronic disease.

The victims, of course, were the young people who were not able to get a good education. Teachers were not paid on time and so frequently went on strike. Salaries of parents were not paid for up to six months, so a lot of students dropped out and went to join the rebel forces that are now destroying the country.

Sheku Syl Kamara, Sierra Leone

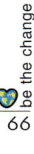

When the new authorities came into power in San Martín de Porres county, the first thing they had to deal with was piles and piles of rubbish building up in the streets. The previous governors had stolen the money allocated to pay the sanitation workers' salaries.

Osver Polo Carreras, Perú

(Corruption is everywhere in my country. Our government is spending tens of millions of dollars on the war in Congo, but they denied it until a newspaper leaked proof. They then admitted the lie but carried on as though nothing had happened.)

Fenni Shangula, Namibia

"Not very long ago, the president of the Pension Administration Office in Bolivia, with the help of some corrupt public officials, stole money from these funds. The most affected were poor people who were saving money for their retirement, cent by cent.
An honest judge revealed, to the authorities and the public, the fraud done. Instead of getting support from the government and his superiors, he was suspended. This shows how corrupt our governmental and judicial systems are. Even when somebody is trying to stop these actions, they get punished.
Carlos Javier Paredes Torrez, Bolivia

We have a poor and corrupt democracy in South Africa. Since 1994, the crime rate has risen to be one of the highest in the world. A woman is raped every 20 seconds. Prisons are overflowing and child abuse is steadily increasing, but this is being ignored. Women and homosexuals are being denied rights. The churches want homosexuality to be made an illegal act, and women are being denied abortions even after they have been raped.
Nina Kettle, South Africa

Corruption is a scourge that knows no boundaries. More and more, it enters every field of our existence—from politics, to business, to health care, to education and even family life. How can we conquer it?
Richard Ngoni, Zambia

CONCLUSION

Corruption only came up in essays from Africa and South America, but it is present everywhere, from pork-barrel politics in the USA to the financial scandals that seem to erupt everywhere. Corruption and poverty are Siamese twins linked at the hip: they feed off each other. Unless both are eradicated, both will blight the lives of our generation. We know how difficult solutions are. We saw real fear creep into the faces of our African friends as they began to recount the scandals that everyone is aware of in their countries—but no one talks about. In an atmosphere of fear generated by oppressive governments that do not allow a free press, corruption grows like a cancer. Again, we believe that education is a key; but when teachers are not paid by the state—or are paid too little—they float through their lessons, giving their best efforts to private paying pupils who come to them after school. In that way, young people learn the power of corruption at an early age. So get integrity into the school system, and use schools as a base from which to pound on the doors of governments and business to create integrity in the rest of society. The question for us is, "Will you turn a blind eye to corruption? Or will we be the generation that fights bravely to end corruption in our lifetimes?"
The Editors

(There must be a free and fearless press; a controlled press never feels sufficiently free to expose and denounce corruption in high places.)
Aminu Seidu, Ghana

Priorities

$Economy

To be without a job is a miserable condition for young people: it was really the only economic issue that our young delegates wanted to talk about. But the issue of inequality and developing world debt came up as a priority in several countries. We all know that a prosperous, fair world economy is a high priority.

> Debt is a ball and chain which poor countries should not be forced to drag into the new millennium.

National debt is a downward spiral. Many countries are in so much debt, they have to borrow more money to make the interest payments—and so they get even deeper into debt. This is an absurd situation, and the downward spiral continues. Debt has made most of the countries lose hope in their economic development. Jubilee 2000 has recommended that the rich world's best millennium gift to the poor would be to forgive the debt, and there has been some movement on relieving the debt to the world's poorest countries. But we, like Jubilee 2000, should not cease the fight until the crippling burden of debt is taken off the back of the world's poor forever.

Right now, a large percentage of the money that developing world countries earn is handed straight back to rich countries to pay off interest. If all debts were written off, these countries would be able to improve appalling living conditions. It is the first step in the development of a fair global economy, which all of us want to see in our lifetimes.

Composed from submissions by Isabella Martin Katherine Hall, 52

Unemployment

Unemployment is the scourge of young Africans. In Ghana, they say 62% of the population is unemployed: it's worse for young people. Left with nothing to do, young girls fall into prostitution and boys get into thieving and sometimes murder. Parents get angry because, after spending so much on education, they expect their children to get jobs when they leave school.

It's ridiculous to have unemployment in Africa: there is so much work to do. The real problem is that there is so little money in government to pay for these things. Perhaps the education system should train job creators rather than job seekers. Governments need to encourage co-operatives and provide funds for small businesses, especially for women. If people start getting wages, governments can draw in taxes which can be used to improve healthcare, develop infrastructure, clean up the environment, and improve education. Jobs are the start of everything.

Compiled from essays by Nakgudde Constance, Uganda; Anusha Jogi, Zimbabwe; and Peter Kainu, Kenya

> We have to run our world according to Nature's ecosystems not humanity's ego-systems. Maurice Strong, Mentor

Can(ada) do better!

More than 10% of the people are unemployed here in Canada. The effects on us all are devastating. About 40% of the children live below the poverty line. People on Unemployment Insurance (UI) are blamed by politicians who openly accuse them of cheating and being lazy. In Toronto, 61% of the jobs were lost. Can you honestly tell me that 149,000 Toronto citizens decided life was better on U.I. or welfare?

The governments have changed many things which, it seems to me, ensure that the poor stay poor and the rich get richer. Besides the obvious affects of living in poverty, people are left feeling even more useless and unwanted. Sure the government offers lots of different options to re-educate yourself, but who wants to become in debt to student loans when they are middle-aged or older? Even if you do get a higher education or change your career to keep up, there are still not enough jobs for everyone. And do you really feel better being unemployed and educated? I think I would feel worse.

Sure there are low-paid jobs out there, but how can you raise a family on $6.85/hour? You cannot, and this affects everyone, not just the unemployed. Our crime and divorce rates have gone way up. Kids are dropping out of school because what's the use of getting educated if there are no jobs when you get out of school and you are made to feel like a second-class citizen. I wonder if we laid off 100 of the top-paid politicians and put their wages and expenses into the deficit each year, how many new jobs could we create?! It could be worse. There is a lot of help available in this country for people who lose their jobs and for their children, although it seems a little strange that those on UI benefits are well fed, housed, and clothed while people on low wages paying their taxes live in total poverty.

Of course we're lucky to have what we have: Canada regularly makes it to the top of the Human Development Index, which makes us the most developed country in the world. It's just hard, growing up here, to believe that this is as good as it can get.

Stewart J. Spiers (Canada)

Cameroon

ACTION Plan

To combat the problem of unemployment and lack of job opportunities in Cameroon, members of the Rescue Mission there are planning on setting up an Internet and telephone cabin. The purpose is to familiarize young Cameroonians with the internet and provide them with e-mail addresses. Hopefully, with the increased knowledge gained from the Internet and use of computers, they will be able to secure more stable jobs and improve employment opportunities.

Philippines

ACTION Plan

A group of people have planned a competition through which they can find and endorse adequate tourism locations. They plan to promote tourism in the selected areas throughout the Philippines. Sustainable tourism is their goal. Care of the environment is key in addition to the economic gain.

Sustainable Tourism

Tourism is the world's largest industry, employing directly and indirectly millions of people. It is growing incredibly fast. Many delegates were concerned that we promote sustainable tourism: this will allow us to appreciate natural wonders and works of man while at the same time taking special care of their surrounding natural and human environments so that future generations can enjoy and learn from them.

Michelle Luxon, Canada

Priorities

Democracy
Power to the People

Renza Moniz, Qatar

Democracy came out as the lowest of the top ten priorities of the Congress. It did not make it to the official delegates' list. It was not mentioned at all in the Latin American regional meeting; twenty years ago, it would undoubtedly have been the top priority for all concerned young people. Except for Africa, where it was a hot topic in the regional discussions, most of us take democracy for granted. But we all recognize it as the foundation of a fair and sustainable society.

Regional Views of Democracy

In the North American regional meeting, a code of cooperation was discussed which included the following basic rules:
- Everyone participates.
- Everyone listens to each other.
- It's OK to disagree but everyone is courteous.
- Speeches are brief and focused.
- Creativity and innovation are honored.
- Everyone is solution-oriented rather than problem-oriented.

Randolf Pinaya, Bolivia

In Africa, everyone called for "greater democracy"—but what does that mean? Either you have democracy, or you do not. Many African dictators manipulate democracy to their own ends and say that they govern democratically. But it is a lie. They defend themselves by saying that African democracy should not be ruled by the Western models of democracy, but that is like saying that African truth should not be defined by Western standards of integrity.
We all know that many African politicians habitually buy votes, operate single-party systems, control the press, torture and abuse any individuals who dare to set up opposition parties—and break up their meetings with their police or army forces. This is not democracy—and all Africans have a duty to fight for democracy as they fight for their other human rights. Without it, we shall never have free and fair governments that truly fight against corruption, that allow the free development of the human spirit—both creative and entrepreneurial. Democracy is our only guarantee of peace and prosperity for Africa, and indeed all parts of the world. Fight for it. Demand it.

In Europe, the only discussion of democracy was about democratic participation of those under 18. More effective youth councils must be set up so that the voice of youth can be heard. These national youth councils must be linked to a European youth council so that all youth in Eastern, Central, and Western Europe can be drawn together into a single, powerful voice.

be the change

The Unknown Youth

The Millennium Youth—here he is
Hear his voice—for he has potential
He has power
He is resourceful
He should not be neglected
He should be given love, care, shelter, and education
These are his rights: above all
The right to live, speak out, assemble, and make decisions
Think what he may become if given these rights.
Think what he may become if denied these rights.
Always—think twice. Think of our generation.
The Millennium Youth — as yet unknown and unheard.

Famara Singhata, The Gambia

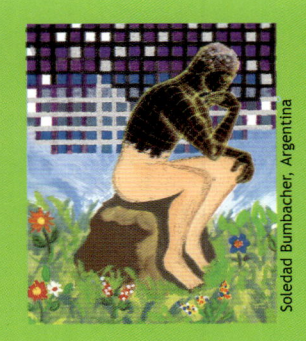

Soledad Bumbacher, Argentina

Democracy: the view of a Bhutanese refugee

Democracy is government of the people, by the people, for the people. Winston Churchill called it the "least awful form of government." Another politician called it "Government limited by the police station and the polling station." In other words, democracy is government that is itself controlled by the rule of law and an independent judiciary and freely elected and/or dismissed by the adult citizenry.

Alas! Though democracy is a fundamental right under the Universal Declaration, there are still some countries, like Bhutan, where democracy is denied. The government asserts that it is unnecessary and "not suitable for a small nation." In Bhutan, democracy is not only denied, it is abhorred.

Bhutan was ruled by a two-tier system of temporal and religious rule up until 1907 when Ugyen Wangchuk, with the help of the British, usurped the throne and set up the kingdom. Jigme Singye Wangchuk, the fourth and, we hope, the last, king of Bhutan has cleverly evicted 100,000 of his people who now live as refugees in Nepal. Why? Because we wanted democracy.

It is instructive for us to watch how the international community takes action in support of democratic self-determination in East Timor or Kosova. In these places, the will of the people is supported. Democracy lives! But no one takes action against the Milosevic of Bhutan—I expect that most of you reading this never even knew there was a problem there.

Democracy cannot be like a private privilege, bought and paid for for the few, but not for others. It must be a universal, basic human right—defended for all. Those that deny it to their citizens must be prosecuted in the international criminal courts and denied their legitimacy as rulers. Can it be done? We think so, and we suffer the miserable existence as refugees, alongside the peoples of Tibet, Kurdistan, Western Sahara, Chechnya, Western Papua and other places believing that one day democracy will live in our nations and we shall at last be free.

Democracy may indeed be a low priority for those of you that enjoy it, but for those of us that do not, it is the basic, indeed the only, priority. Please help us my friends. We want to go back to our motherland as free, independent citizens of a Bhutanese democracy. As long as one country is denied free, democratic rule, we are all the poorer. Please, let our generation be the one that brings universal democratic rule to our world.

Sukman Tamang, 16, Bhutan (though living now in this refugee camp in Nepal)

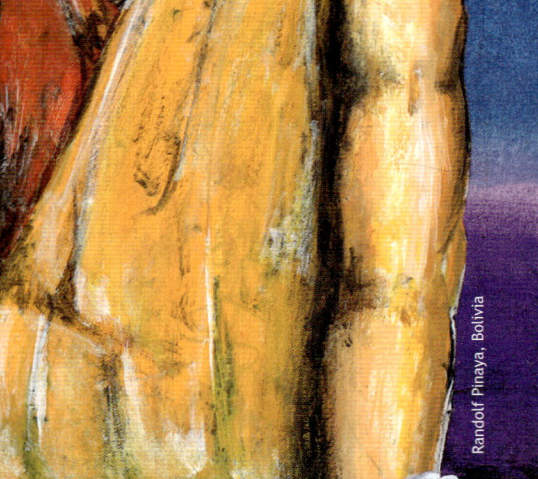

Randolf Pinaya, Bolivia

Priorities

Animal Rights

Animal experiments are unacceptable because scientists put animals through a tremendous amount of painful suffering in order to research new medicines and test products made for humans. These animals are locked in cages, just waiting for the time when they will be pulled out and tortured, poked and prodded, and usually killed. Some animals are not given anesthetics to minimize the pain, which shows the total lack of ethics and compassion of the scientist. They have absolutely no interest in how much pain this animal will go through. Animals are force-fed with toxic chemicals and burned by lotions and creams rubbed on their shaved skin. When the Japanese and Germans used human beings for medical experiments during the World War II, they were prosecuted as homicidal monsters. Now, as scientists daily use animals to test cosmetics, drugs, and household goods, we barely complain. If it was the other way around, and animals tested their products on humans, certainly this practice would come to a swift end.

Morgan Woolley, Hawaii

The Animal Kingdom - a kingdom we should never rule

It does not matter whether or not you believe animals have souls. It does not matter if you don't believe they can reason. The only thing that matters is that these animals can suffer ... and they do daily ... and needlessly. We must help these animals. Isn't the happiness of animals worth a little of your time?

Note found in the Small Island States Regional Discussion room

Humans can be pretty horrible animals. We hunt for sport, watch bullfights and rooster fights for fun. It is a terrible way for human beings to make money and entertain themselves. Right now, in the UK, there is a big debate about banning fox hunting. Hundreds of intelligent people are fighting to keep this massacring of small animals legal. In these activities, humans are the monsters and the animals are the poor victims. Let's hope our generation can evolve beyond them. There is no need for them.

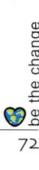

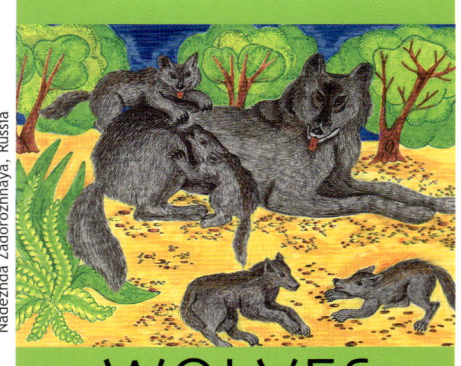

WOLVES

A lot of people didn't just kill wolves; they tortured them. They set wolves on fire, tore their jaws out, cut their Achilles tendons, and turned dogs loose on them. They poisoned them with strychnine, arsenic, and cyanide on such a scale that millions of other animals—racoons, black-footed ferrets, red foxes, ravens, red-tailed hawks, eagles, ground squirrels, wolverines—were killed incidentally in the process ... a sad testament to our lack of ethics and compassion. Our reputation of understanding and respect for non-human life is virtually non-existent. It cries out for repair. The sooner we begin to listen to that small voice within us that valiantly continues to set the truth before our eyes, the sooner we will be able to step up another rung on the ladder of evolution. If our generation is to learn anything at all from this history, it is that we must find a way to broaden our circle of understanding to include all the beings with whom we share this lovely earth and strengthen our responsibility to both ourselves and to our Earth Mother's other children.

Barry Holston Lopez
"Of Wolves and Men"

The Red Book list of endangered species grows daily. White tigers, koala bears, white rhino, tigers, panda bears, blue whales, polar bears, and hawkbill turtles are only a few of the animals which are on the brink of extinction.

It is crucial to understand that the loss of any one of these precious animals will disrupt our ecosystem and change it forever. We can never bring back the Dodo —and the natural progression will ensure that the last animal to become extinct will be us!

VIVISECTION

There will always be the necessity to develop medicine, cure diseases, and research new kinds of drugs, but there is absolutely NO need to cut up live animals in the development process. It is cruel, inhumane, and totally unnecessary to subject these poor animals to our hypothetical guesses and unfounded experiments. Who gave us the right to torture and kill another living creature? Let ours be the first generation to outlaw this completely in our world.

In starting the Harmony Foundation, I wanted to promote three harmonies: harmony between humans, harmony within humans— between mind and spirit—and harmony between humans and the natural world.

Fred Matser, The Netherlands

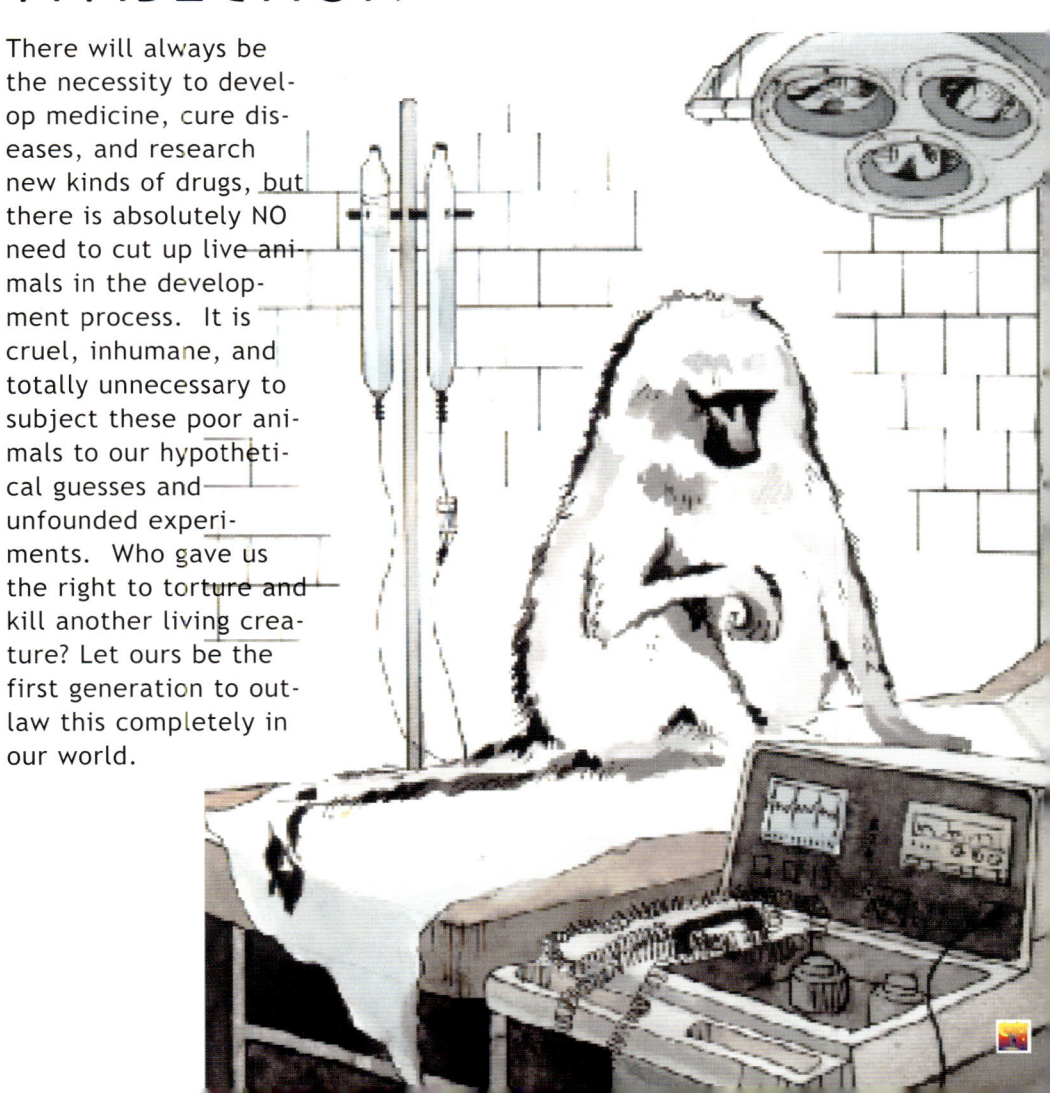

Other Priorities

Many priorities discussed at the Congress didn't make the top ten. Drugs and substance abuse were priorities that came up for many. These are some of the others:

Youth participation
On the next page, we outline ideas that came up at the Congress for greater youth participation in governance at all levels. Until the views of young people are heard in society, few of these other issues will be fully addressed. Getting a school council and a local town youth council is an essential first step.

Teen pregnancy
"Children having children" is still a problem. We feel we can combat it through educating young people about contraception and the effect that having children has on their lives. But adults must help by outlawing infant marriages, making time in school for serious, youth-directed sex education. Prissy, patronizing sex ed. is embarrassing and doesn't work.

Homelessness
Homelessness is a vicious cycle: to get a job, you need a home; to get a home, you need money; to get money, you need a job. Homeless shelters and basic health and food supplies are an absolute must for homeless people.

Nationalism
In the European meeting, delegates worried that their countries are becoming over-run with American TV, clothing, food, and a bland, global mono-culture. For many delegates, restoring national pride through teaching young people their cultural heritage is a high priority.

Child prostitution
In parts of Asia and Africa, you find young men and women being prostituted, many against their own will. This must stop. It is dangerous not only because of the impact it will have on the young person's life, but because it spreads diseases like AIDS—which could wipe out whole swathes of the economically productive population.

Domestic violence
One of our mentors, Orlan Bishop, told us that domestic violence is the number one cause of child and female injury in the USA. It has to be stopped, and it is young men who have to lead the way *(but never forget that much domestic violence on children is done by women)*. Not only does it cause physical injury, but deep emotional scars remain that will affect generation after generation.

Child molestation
This disturbing and cruel crime is a horrendous violation of a young person's dignity and self-respect. Many people would like to see a much more severe punishment for the offenders and a larger support network for the victims.

Homophobia
Many delegates are concerned with homophobia—fear of homosexuals. In South Africa, the church is lobbying to make homosexuality illegal. The only solution is to educate people: everybody is the same, no matter what their sexual orientation.

ODE TO A FRIEND LOST TO DRUGS

Tears fill my eyes,
And roll down my cheek.
As I say my last goodbyes,
To you lying before me,
So frail and weak.

As your eyes shut,
And you fall asleep,
My grief is immeasurable,
I cannot help but weep.

I travel back in time,
To our days of fun and laughter;
Of fighting, of squabbling,
And uniting again after.

I tried to convince you,
That drugs weren't cool.
But you just looked at me,
And thought I was a fool.

You hated me for saying,
That drugs weren't right.
And when I refused to take them,
We got into a fight.

I had to be stupid,
I had to be dumb.
To refuse to do something,
That was so much fun.

Today you've left me,
Totally on my own.
It's really hard to live,
Like this, all alone.

Your life was too short,
Of much consequence, to be
But your death has taught plenty
At least to me.

As pain sears through my heart,
In this period of strife,
I'm glad I gave up being cool,
And, in return got my life!

Aditi Rao, India

Substance Abuse

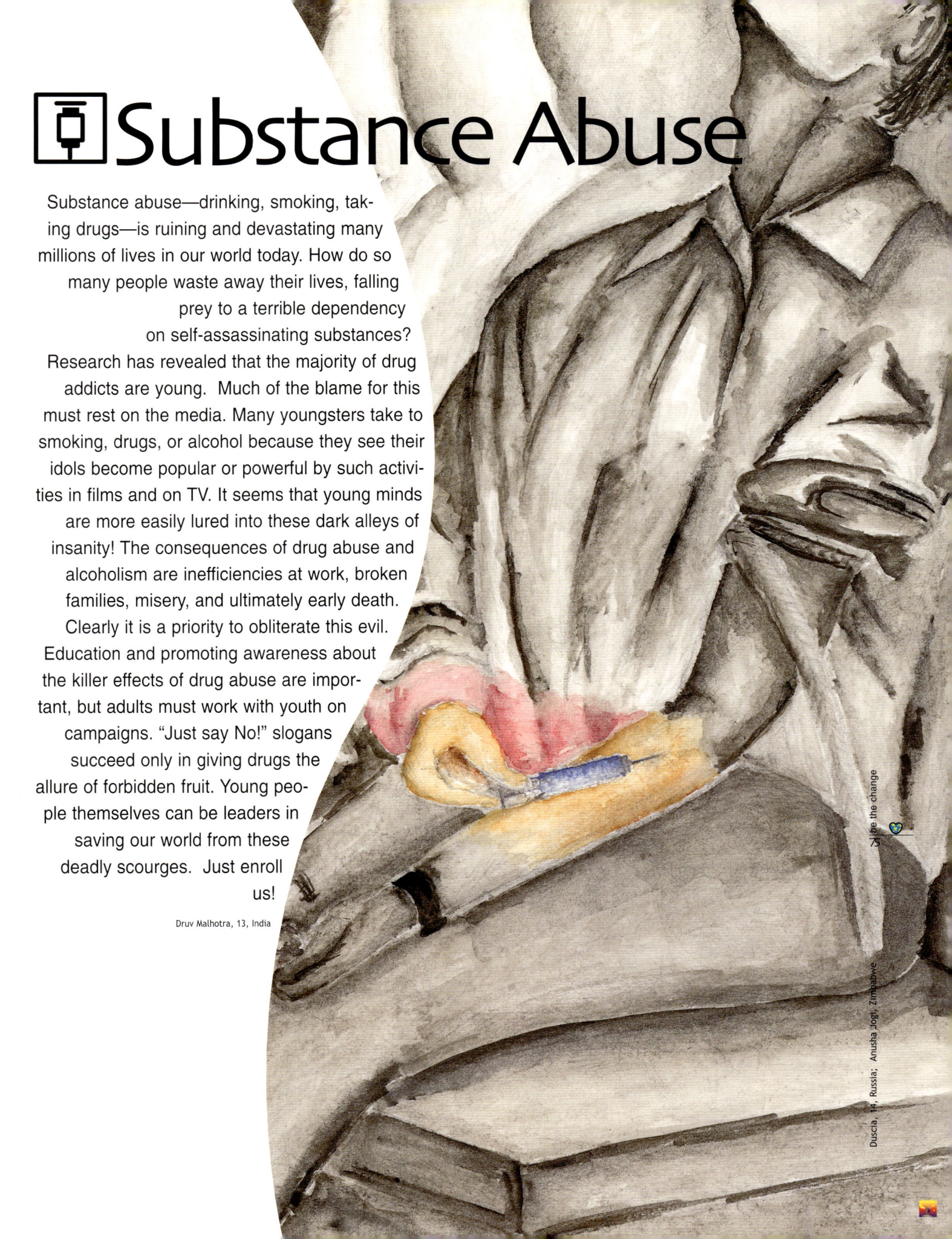

Substance abuse—drinking, smoking, taking drugs—is ruining and devastating many millions of lives in our world today. How do so many people waste away their lives, falling prey to a terrible dependency on self-assassinating substances? Research has revealed that the majority of drug addicts are young. Much of the blame for this must rest on the media. Many youngsters take to smoking, drugs, or alcohol because they see their idols become popular or powerful by such activities in films and on TV. It seems that young minds are more easily lured into these dark alleys of insanity! The consequences of drug abuse and alcoholism are inefficiencies at work, broken families, misery, and ultimately early death. Clearly it is a priority to obliterate this evil. Education and promoting awareness about the killer effects of drug abuse are important, but adults must work with youth on campaigns. "Just say No!" slogans succeed only in giving drugs the allure of forbidden fruit. Young people themselves can be leaders in saving our world from these deadly scourges. Just enroll us!

Druv Malhotra, 13, India

Duscia, 14, Russia; Anusha Jogi, Zimbabwe

"Todos somos iguales no

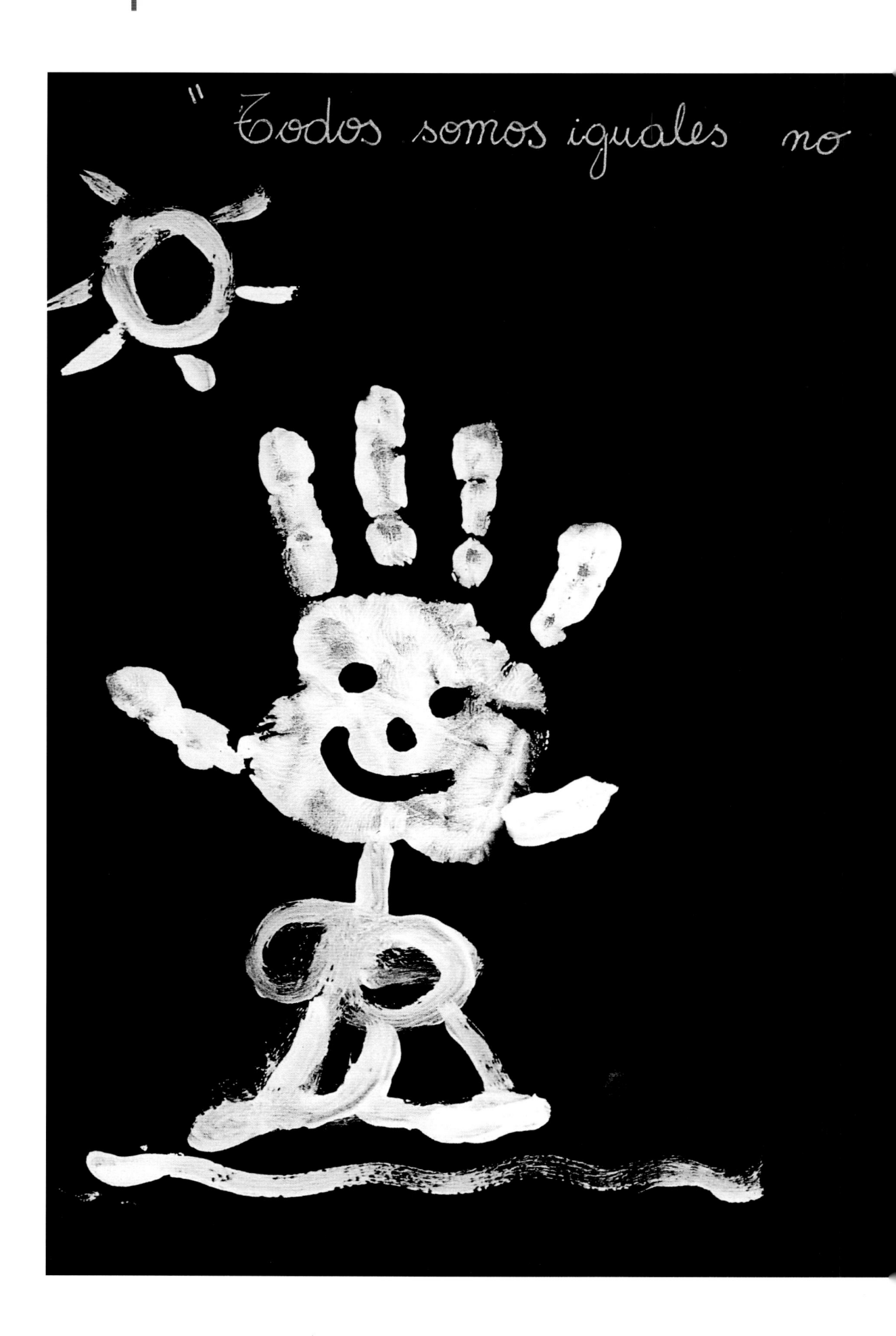

"importa' nuestro color"

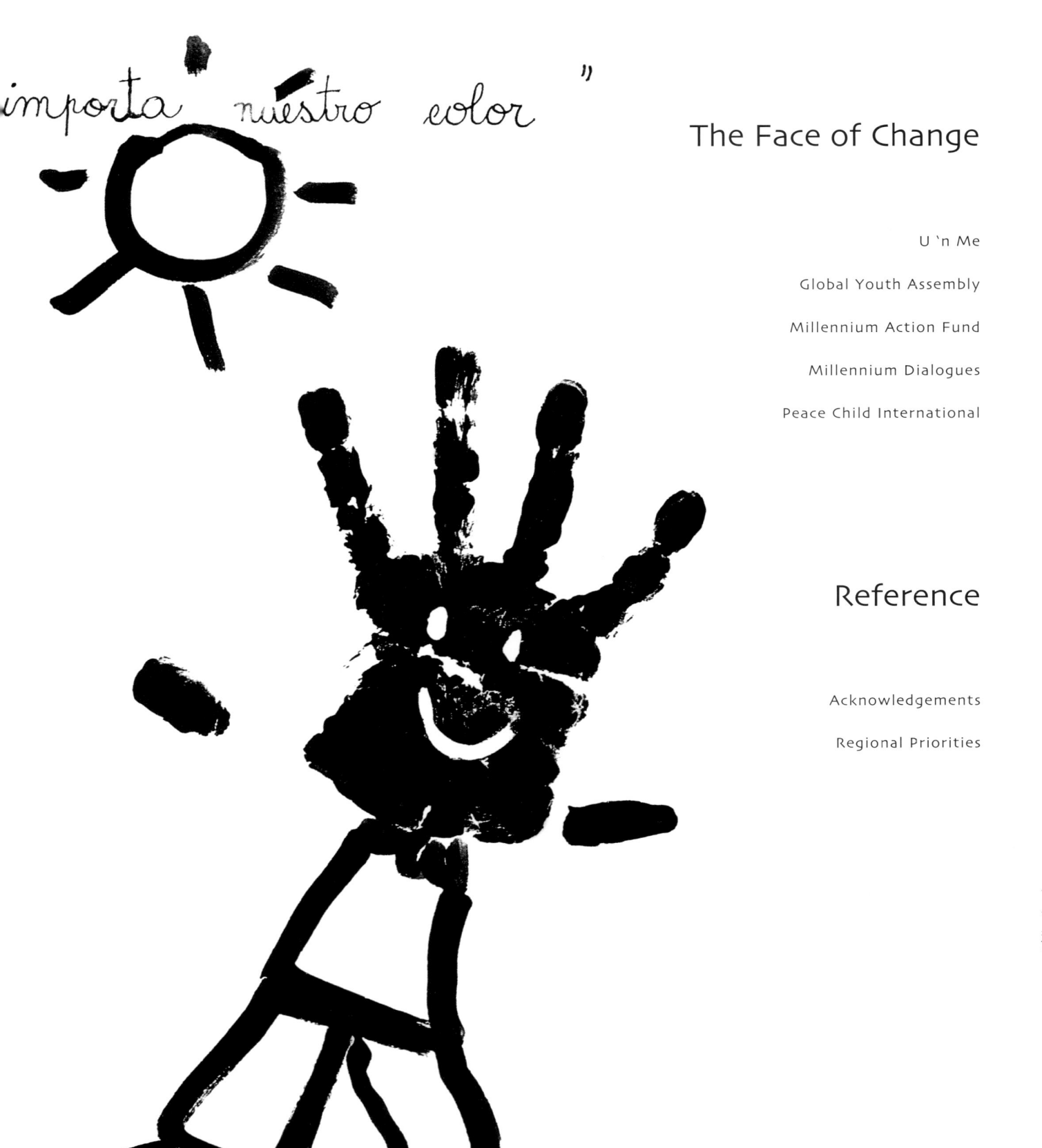

The Face of Change

U 'n Me

Global Youth Assembly

Millennium Action Fund

Millennium Dialogues

Peace Child International

Reference

Acknowledgements

Regional Priorities

be the change
77

Priorities

> *Any one who thinks that small things cannot make a big difference in your life has never spent a night in a room with a mosquito.*
> — Hunter Lovins, MYPC mentor

U 'n Me: UN & Youth

Based on an original proposal by Danijela Zunec from Croatia.

1. Background

At a UNESCO youth meeting at the United Nations in New York, two young people were riding up the elevator in the main Secretariat building and saw that there was no stop on the 28th floor. On the way down, they stopped at the 29th and walked down. The 28th floor is a vast, empty space with just air-conditioning and heating pipes.

A vision hit them like lightning: an entire floor at the heart of the UN given over to young people! It would be dedicated to communicating the passion and idealism of the UN to young people around the world in a multitude of languages via phone, fax, newsletters, e-mails, and of course most important—the Internet.

2. Need

The UN is beleaguered. With non-payment of dues by it's richest members plus very public upstaging in international peace-keeping by NATO, it is losing the battle for the hearts and minds of the people who wept tears of joy at its creation more than 50 years ago. Youth love the idea of the UN—the work that it does and the global community that it represents. We can see the need for a stronger UN in the future to defend individual human rights, protect the environment, ensure world peace, encourage human development, and nurture a more cohesive world family. But too often the effort that the UN puts into getting the attention of youth are ineffective, patronizing, unimaginative, and lacking follow-up. Fifty percent of the world's population is under 25: the UN must harness their energy and idealism in its mission and enable them to give more help in the battle for a stronger UN in the 21st century.

3. Summary

Our purpose is to create a home at the heart of the UN for young people from which to communicate UN work to youth outside, and our purpose is to provide a channel for youth perspectives on UN initiatives on the inside.

4. Project Outline

Danijela proposed a partnership deal with the UN: they provide the space, the stationery, the phone lines, the desks, the printing, photocopying, and postage stamps. In return, a coalition of NGOs will provide the young people—their accommodation, flights and living expenses—plus the adult management. This group would be answerable to a UN-

Duncan Richard, Tanzania

appointed Governing Body within the UN Department of Public Information.

For the first six months, six to ten young people and an adult "manager" would design an outreach program around a weekly e-mail update and a bi-monthly magazine —all in the six UN languages. They would also produce an annual youth state of the world report, detailing the major environmental, human rights, security, inequality, and job problems, with the UN responses to them.

In the second six months, the number of students and outreach projects would increase to include other languages—German, Japanese, Portuguese, Hindi, Urdu, Kiswahili, etc. The young staff would guarantee to respond to all youth inquiries within 24 hours using policy guidelines approved by UN adult staff. The unit will also provide a considered youth response to any official UN policy issue within seven days.

After five years, we would like to see the project grow to involve 60 to 70 young people working as volunteers for 12-month periods on the UN Youth Floor, circulating outreach in 30+ languages and injecting massive amounts of youth energy, commitment, and drive into all work the UN does, providing whole new areas of support from NGOs and—in particular—schools where millions of young people wait, hoping for someone to engage them.

5. People & Organizations

Peace Child International will try to work with most of the organizations, delegates, and activists gathering for the Millennium Young Peoples Congress plus any other youth-led organizations which want to be involved.

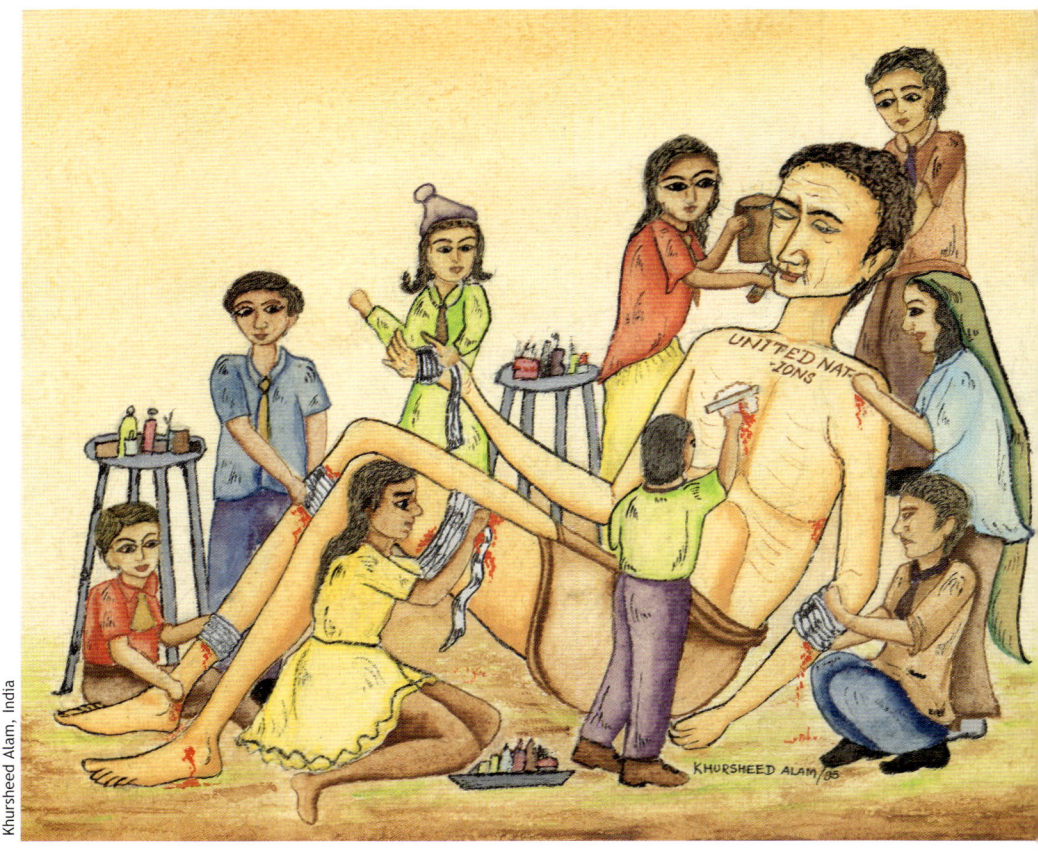

"Binding the wounds of the United Nations"

6. Budget

We estimate that the cost of about one year is around $100,000 for the UN and a similar amount to cover the expenses of the youth volunteers: a total of $200,000—.17% of the total budget of the UN Department of Public Information. Surely, a worthwhile investment to secure support of the generation on which the UN's future depends.

7. Evaluation

The project will be evaluated by UN member states in the General Assembly. Objectively verifiable measures of its success should include: the numbers of people contacting the Unit for information, the extent of the mailing list, the quality of the publications, the e-mail updates and the quality of youth input to UN initiatives when requested.

This proposal was used in the Congress briefing papers to show young people how to prepare their action plans which each delegate had to bring to Hawaii. WE ENCOURAGE EVERY READER TO FOLLOW THIS FORMAT AND SEND US A PROPOSAL FOR ADDRESSING ANY OF THE PRIORITIES DISCUSSED IN THIS BOOK AND OTHERS THAT WE SHOULD HAVE GOT AROUND TO.

Global Youth Assembly

Imagine a world where the voices of youth are heard. A place where people like you and me can meet and have an impact. Can you imagine what it would be like to have a seat at the UN and in governments influencing their decisions? Just think, if we had such a structure, we could change our world! So what are we waiting for? Go for it — BE THAT CHANGE!

This is the face of that change. It is a structure to enable us to accomplish that idea. Albert Einstein said that if the world is to survive the 21st century it must develop two things: one of them is a world youth parliament. Our plan meets this objective.

UN Millennium Assembly

The idea of a Global Youth Assembly (GYA) was first raised by Peace Child's in Rescue Mission in 1993. At the Congress, Peaceways promoted their UN Youth General Assembly idea while Youth in Action presented the Global Youth Assembly. Essentially, they are all the same thing — a permanent World Youth Assembly meeting every two to three years composed of youth representatives from national and international youth-led organizations — groups like Peace Child International, Boy Scouts, Girl Guides, wildlife clubs, young people's parliaments like that set up in Mongolia, and other international meetings — like those organized by UNESCO and UNEP. The criterion for inclusion is that each must enable the voice of youth to be freely heard.

The first meeting will be before the UN's Millennium Assembly so that young people can reach a consensus on their message to leaders. Thereafter, it should meet every two to three years in different locations around the world — such as Morocco in 2003 — to discuss global issues concerning youth and to decide action strategies to address them.

$$$ for Action

A central facet of the GYA structure is to have the funds to enable youth to take action. The Millennium Action Fund (MAF) will be hopefully one of many funds to supply up-front funding for youth-led projects. The Youth In Action Awards (YIAA) is a similar youth-led structure set up to give financial awards to those who have completed excellent action projects. Peace Child laid down a challenge to governments and development organizations: "If you want education for all and an end to poverty, give 5% of your development aid to projects led by that 50% of the world's population that is under 25." Five percent for the 50% seems like a fair deal! In fact, it is more than 2 billion dollars, so you can see that it is a long-term target. But one day young people may well prove to be the most effective engines of development.

Outreach and Promotion

The mouthpiece is a way for young people to promote important information about activities and global issues to their peers around the world. In our vision, the hub would be located at the United Nations, where the U 'n Me idea will set up a youth-run office containing representatives from different regions — Asia, Africa, small island states etc. Working with a network of youth centers around the world like the Peace Child International Center in the UK, their job would be to produce

The Hair:
Youth-led NGOs and civil society organizations and official national youth advisory councils. As numerous as the hairs on your head!

The Mouth:
The promotion and outreach section: young people speaking out about what they do and what they need to their peers and everyone else. The tongue is what we will use to tickle governments and the UN — and to stick out at them if we feel they are compromising our future.

The Brain:
The Global Youth Assembly itself where representatives of all these groups meet and establish policies and goals.

The Eyes:
Funding sources: to date we have in mind just the MAF and the YIAA, but there should be many more sources. Youth need a thousand eyes!

The Feedback Loop:
Through discussion and promotion, more young people and organizations will be recruited, thus feeding the brain with new ideas and initiatives.

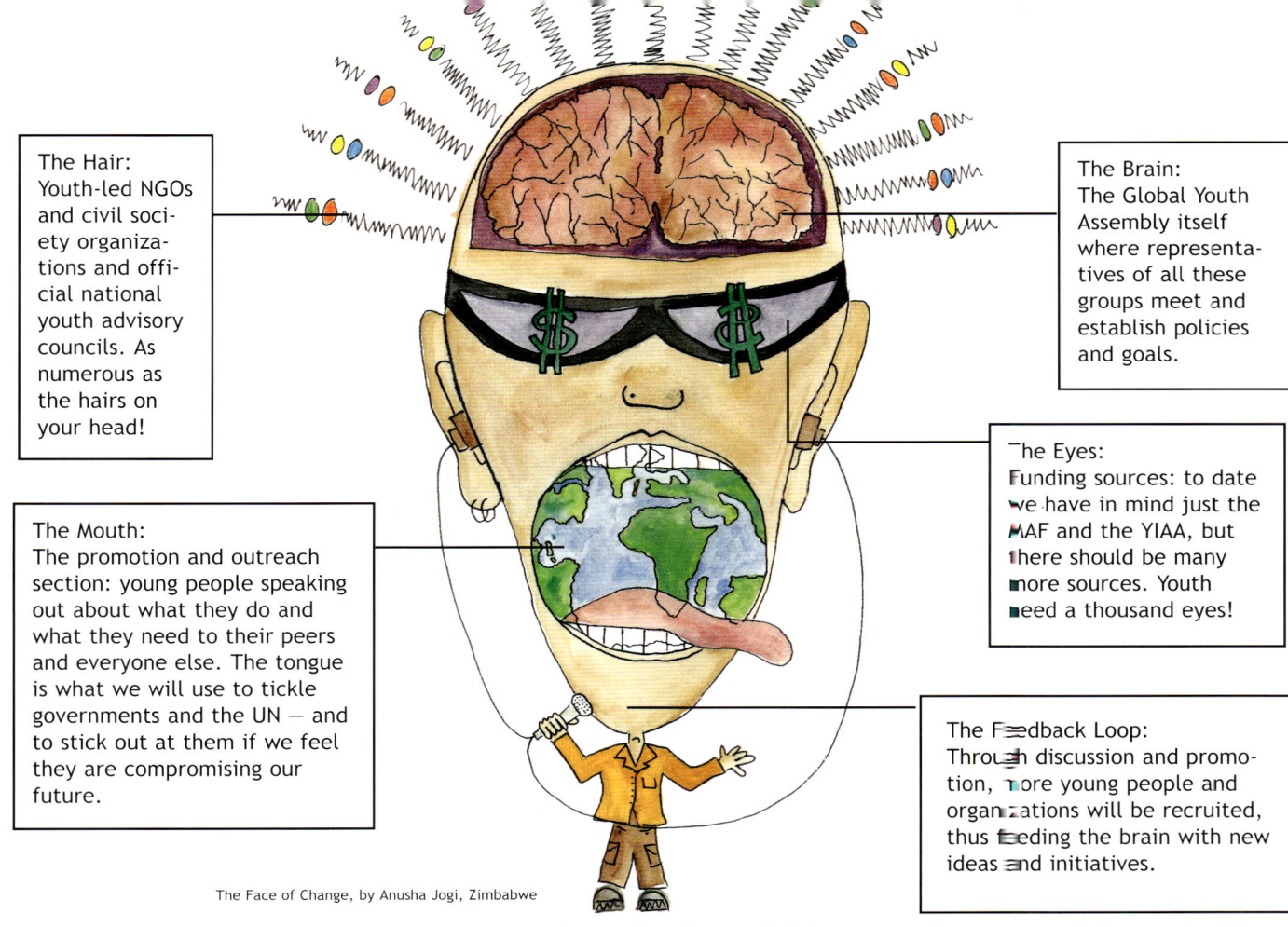

The Face of Change, by Anusha Jogi, Zimbabwe

books and newsletters and to update Internet web pages to keep these groups and all young people supplied with information about what the UN is doing and what youth are accomplishing.

Government Outreach

Outreach to governments and the United Nations is the vital road to power, so we shall lobby every government and UN agency to establish youth advisory councils. In this way, young people can take part in local and national decision-making about their future. This was promised in Agenda 21 and many other agreements our governments have signed. They are not going to fulfill those agreements unless we show them first how to do it, and second, prove to them that we can be useful to them.

Craig Kielburger, founder of the excellent Free the Children group, recommends that young people have a seat on the Security Council. Why not? We fully support and endorse this initiative.

Staffed by Young People

Almost all of the work for the GYA structure could be done by young people — teenagers aged 13 to 20. Adults would work in partnership with us, as they do in the Peace Child center. They are certainly helpful in areas like fundraising, gaining access to people, etc.

As far as possible, though, a completely youth-run setup would be the goal. After all, adults have their own groups, but it would be great if we could all work together. Youth and adults working together to change and improve the world to be a better place would be awesome. We need a better way to confront the problems of our world - most of which we created. But, as we made the problems, they shouldn't be that hard to solve! All we need to do is share our ideas and energy, and TAKE ACTION!!

MOROCCO 2003

The last action taken by the Millennium Young People's Congress was to accept an invitation by the Government of Morocco to hold a follow-up Congress in 2003.

Hopefully this will be a full-dress meeting of the Global Youth Assembly — but whatever happens with this initiative, we see this as an opportunity to review our progress on our action plans, and the development of National Youth Advisory Councils.

Many dreams were generated during the build-up to this Congress and during the Congress itself. Morocco 2003 is our chance to see how many of them have been realized. **Thanks, Morocco, for giving us this target to work towards!**

Millennium Action Fund

From the very first discussions, the MYPC Steering Committee decided that what would distinguish this Congress from almost all others would be the quality of the follow-up. So we challenge everyone to have a Millennial Dialogue with your leaders *(see next page)* and harangue them with your priorities… - But what then? What will you do to translate some of the dreams in this book into realities?

As part of the criteria for coming to the congress, participants were required to hand in at the Airport upon arrival Action Proposals, outlining a plan for what they, individually, were going to do to address the Congress priorities when they get home. Nearly 300 Action Plans were collected, more than half of which are very well thought out, costed and scheduled. Most are seeking between $250 and $1,000 US dollars to get started – and we hope to raise between $50- $100,000 to give out at our first distribution in May 2000.

The Fund is open to all youth-led projects, not just those submitted by Congress delegates and activists. So if you are a young person with a project that you are burning to get started which will address any of the issues you have read about in these pages, please go ahead and send it to the address at the end of the facing page.

We found it useful to have all the Action Proposals follow the same format, thus:
1. Summary Proposal - a short description of the project;
2. Background - a description of your group and/ or yourself and the context for the project
3. Need - - what particular need or problem is being addressed by your project
4. Detailed Proposal – a detailed description of the work you will undertake if you get the grant;
5. Budget – detailed breakdown of all the costs involved, and how much you are asking from the MAF;
6. Biographies and Contact Information – who are you, and why are you the best possible people to do this project?
7. Mentors - letter of intent and contact information for adult mentor(s)
8. Evaluation - details on who will independently evaluate the project and a list of objectively measurable indicators to assess whether or not the project has successfully addressed the need identified in item 3.

Sheku Syl Kamara, MAF representative for Africa, answers questions

Who will operate the MAF?
The Fund will be led by a steering committee composed of the six regional representatives elected by the Congress - Mia Handshin, Small Island States; Sheku Syl Kamara, Africa; Hassan al Saleh, Asia; Marina Mansilla Herman, Latin America; Sara Cunningham, North America; and Azer Bairamov, Europe; as well as representatives of Peace Child International and other adult advisors. Action Proposals will be reviewed in the first instance by national coordinators and by the regional desk officers at the Peace Child International Centre in England who will short-list the best ones, and get further details on individual plans as they feel necessary. They will then be posted on the MAF website so that everyone can see what everyone else is up to - and the MAF Committee can study the proposals in detail. As we get going, we expect that most dis-

cussions about projects will be handled over the web so the committee will only need to meet once a year. Also, we expect many people will submit their proposals via the web.

We have faith that young people will deliver on ambitious development projects - just as they have delivered books and magnificent musical performances for Peace Child in the past.

There will be several checks and balances. First, our fantastic network of national coordinators: we know they will only recommend projects from the best young people. Second, each project will have an adult mentor who will advise and assist the young people in implementing projects. Third, the Peace Child desk officers will also work to ensure the projects' success.

Peace Child staff will handle the practical distribution of funds and monitor the implementation of each project.

And last, but not least, the Peace Child Charitable Trust and the Millennium Action Fund(USA) will act as financial agents to ensure that funds are used solely for charitable purposes.

What kind of project will get funds?

In order to receive MAF support, projects must:

- be approved by majority vote of the MAF steering committee, by the national coordinator in the country of origin, by the PCI secretariat desk officer, and by the project mentor
- be submitted by young people aged less than 25
- seek amounts between $50 (minimum) and $5,000 (maximum)
- have verifiable measures of achievement by which they may be evaluated
- address one of the priorities agreed to by the Millennium Young People's Congress and have a sustainability component where appropriate
- have an experienced and committed adult mentor
- be submitted in 8-point format Sustainability is an important criteria as well.

We look forward to hearing what you want to do. A fund like this is set up to fund surprise things – things that we will not think of. Things that *you* feel are necessary to sustain life through the 21st Century and the 3rd Millennium. That is what this Congress was all about and the MAF will reflect that goal.

Simon Ndonye, Kenya

Vision of a hi-tech future for Africa!

Send your Action Proposals to:
The Millennium Action Fund, The White House, BUNTINGFORD, Herts UK SG9 9AH

Millenium Dialogues

We urge you to arrange a series of Millennial Dialogues with leaders at every level of your government and civil society. The Millennium Young People's Congress was the climax of one of the largest global reviews of young people's opinions ever conducted in history. Now that they have spoken — now that we have learned what their priorities are at the threshold of this new millennium — it is time to discuss these priorities with our leaders.

Why a Millennial Dialogue? What might young people realistically expect to get out of such a dialogue?
1. Some answers: It would be very interesting to hear why the leaders of nuclear powers like the United Kingdom, France, and others feel that they need to hang on to such weapons in the new millennium. And why — if it would only cost an additional $40 billion a year to feed, clothe, house, educate, and provide clean water and primary health care for the poorest billion on the planet — are we unable to find it? It is less than .2% of our 23 trillion dollar world economy!
2. Some commitments: A commitment to another meeting might be the most you could get out of it. More and more governments are recognizing the value that young people can have in society if they are given some responsibilities. Peer-to-peer counseling is but one example. Many corporations now recognize the value of a youth advisory board; many town councils now have a youth council; some governments are setting up structures to introduce youth advice at every level, thus "involving young people in decision-making," as every major UN conference from the Rio Earth Summit onward promised. But governments are still fairly clueless about how to do this: a Millennial Dialogue can discuss and brainstorm what might be the best way for your country.
3. Some discussion: Since young people have, in their infinite wisdom, determined that education is the number one priority going into the new millennium, it is surely worthwhile for governments to discuss, face-to-face, with the recipients — or victims — of the current educational systems how they might be improved. What might 'mandatory student involvement in all aspects of curriculum planning and assessment look like? How can students educate themselves about subjects like sustainable development that are not part of the formal curricula and which their teachers are not trained to teach? How do you teach peace, human rights, and population control? And how can young people themselves help governments reach their Jomtien goal of "education for all," given that, on their own, they failed to meet their target of achieving it by the year 2000?

What do you need for a Millennial Dialogue?
1. A media partner such as a TV station, newspaper, or magazine. You stand a far, far better chance of getting to meet someone important if you present it like a request by a journalist for an interview. Also, the results of the dialogue will be much more widely read. So choose a youth-friendly news-paper, show them this book, and invite them to be your media sponsor with first-run rights on the dialogue.
2. An appointment: First choose your target(s). Discuss with your media partner who will be the best value and who will be most youth-friendly. It could be the head of state, a cabinet minister, the head of a council, the chief executive of a big corporation. Think long and hard about whom you would like to have your Millennial Dialogue with. Then go through your target's press office and set up the appointment. Also, talk to your parents, teachers, and friends as there is often someone who knows someone who went to school with your target or who knows how to get to them.
2. A theme: It is important to define a theme for your dialogue. You can make it very general, like "The role of youth in society" — which allows you to talk about just about anything — or you can focus on your top priorities: education, peace, human rights. Let your target know the theme of your discussion ahead of time so that they can prepare. Make a long list of questions that you would like to ask, then whittle them down to the

really important ones that reach toward your goal. Be very strategic and plot the course of your discussion in as much detail as possible, while allowing sufficient flexibility to enable the discussion to range over issues that you might not have thought of.

3. Goals: It's as well to have several goals going into your discussion. That way you stand a better chance of getting something out of the dialogue. One goal should be a follow-up meeting; another might be a letter of endorsement for one of your action plans. Better would be a solid commitment of cash for the Millennium Action Fund. One goal that we would like to see set for every Millennial Dialogue is to get your government to confirm that it will support the inclusion of a Youth presentation at the UN's Millennium Assembly in September 2000. The UN only does what its member states want. They will allow a youth presentation at this assembly IF enough governments support the idea.

You will know better than we what goals to set for your dialogue. Be sure to include some "yes-able" options: things that your target will find it easy to say "yes!" to.

Timing? Obviously, the sooner you can set up your Millennial Dialogue, the better. However, if you are reading this in 2002 or 2003, there is still time. A millennium is a long period, and we see great value in having Millennial Dialogues about priorities for this one right through 2010 and beyond. The important thing is for the dialogue to be on-going. That is why having an infrastructure that allows young people to meet regularly with officials to discuss common concerns would be so valuable. Try to get one set up in your country, and then such dialogues can happen on a regular (ie., annual?!) basis.

Prasinjya Phukan, Jordan

Peace Child International

International Organizer of the Millennium Young People's Congress

Peace Child's mission is to empower young people. Through its books, musicals, conferences, and internships, it offers young people chances to express their concerns. It operates from a residential center in the UK. Young people from around the world run the office and the projects in partnership with a small adult staff.

There are still too many people who think that young people should be seen and not heard. Peace Child sees young people as highly talented, potentially productive citizens. It exists to harness the energy of young people to drive the changes our world urgently needs.

Here Druv Malhotra outlines Peace Child's history and what it means to him.

Peace Child was founded by David and Rosey Woollcombe in 1981. At that time, relations between the USSR and the USA were not very cordial! David's mother-in-law asked him to do a play to promote peace. David decided to make youth and theater a medium of rapprochement. With David Gordon writing the inspirational music, Peace Child, the musical, was born with young people writing much of the dialogue themselves. The play thus became a powerful platform from which young people might express their views. The play, overflowing with radical ideas and creative energy, spread across the United States and into the Soviet Union. In 1986, Peace Child International managed to organize the first youth exchange between Soviet and American children, creating a spirit of fraternity and concord between the youth of warring nations! Peace Child's mission is Empowering Young People — to give youth an opportunity to shape the world that they shall inherit. It has a history of prolific activity. In 1988, another play "Earth Child" was produced that brought to light rapid environmental degradation. It also pioneered publications by and for young people about social and environmental issues. The first book was called, *Children's State of the Planet Handbook* presenting complex information in

David and Rosey Woollcombe: backbone of Peace Child International

a colorful and stimulating way to appeal to youth. A children's edition of the Rio Earth Summit Agenda 21; a history of the past, present, and future of the United Nations; young people's editions of the Universal Declaration of Human Rights; and the UN Environment Program's Global Environment Outlook followed. All publications are composed of material created by youth and edited by a youth editorial board — like this report.

The Millennium Young People's Congress is the most mammoth project of Peace Child International involving two years of arduous work and all its vast network around the world. Upcoming Peace Child projects include a youth version of the human development report and the development of the Millennium Action Fund.

Peace Child has radically changed my perspectives and widened my horizons. I have decided to adopt its philosophy of optimism towards the problems that plague our world today. I have understood the futility of being cynical about things. I have learnt how each individual's actions have a collective effect on our world. Peace Child has equipped me with the tools that can bring about tangible change. In turn, I shall ignite my fellow youth with the fire of enthusiasm kindled in me by Peace Child when I go back to my country. It's all about inspiration as well as perspiration. The dynamic people at Peace Child inspire us with their youthful energy and creativity to be the change we want to see in the world. And it is up to us to take the inspiration and with our perspiration work toward that change. The people at Peace Child have trusted me as a future leader to go back to my country and bring about reformation. This conviction, this indefatigable trust in me has given me the confidence to take action, the courage to accept failure, and the conviction to remain committed to the cause. Thus I can begin to create the renaissance that I envision and along with fellow youth do something that shall help alleviate our problems. After all, if each one of us decides to change just ourselves, would there not be a global reformation?

Editing this book has been a great learning experience for me. It has enhanced my writing abilities and acquainted me with the perspectives and opinions of other youth. Peace Child International has literally fired me up to be the change!

Dhruv Malhotra

Uylya Uynenko, Russia

Many thanks to the Peace Child MYPC team:
Adam Bien, Project Coordinator; Lindsay Gray & Heather Stabler, Transport Coordinators; Rob James & Erin Mendelson, Hawaii-UK Liaison; David Baines, Africa Desk; Dominique Mansilla Hermann, Latin America Desk; Lissa Wheen, Asia Desk & UK National Coordinator; Tom Jolly & Julian Olivier, UK Transit Liaison; Cecilia Weckström, Logo & Workbook design; Alexander Woollcombe, UK-Hawaii Liaison; Rosey Simonds(Woollcombe), Project Assistant; David Woollcombe, Project Director.

Contact: Peace Child International, The White House, BUNTINGFORD, Herts, UK SG9 9AH
Tel: (44) 176 327 4459; Fax: (44) 176 327 4460;
e-mail: rescuemission@compuserve.com

The Hawaiian Community responds with aloha

The Millennium Host Committee (MHC) was formed in September 1998 to fund and create the support structure, programs, and events of the Millennium Young People's Congress. In less than a year, it had raised close to $1,000,000 in both monetary and in-kind resources from businesses and organizations in Oahu.

The secret to the success of this massive endeavor was the commitment, goodwill, and hard work of a large network of volunteers. The MHC was lucky to have such a group at the heart of its effort. In the months ahead, with leadership from Youth for Environmental Service (YES), we look forward to the development of the Millennium Action Fund and to maintaining contacts with the youth delegates and activists. We commit to assisting Hawaii's youth with action projects based on the MYPC priorities.

Maeona Mendelson, Congress Co-Director; Chief Executive, Millennium Host Committee

Title Sponsor: The State of Hawaii

Diamond Sponsors: United Nations Environment Program (UNEP)
Hawaii Tourism Authority / Hawaii Visitors and Convention Bureau

Platinum Sponsors: Government of the Netherlands
Communications-Pacific, Inc.

Millennium Television Network - Humanities Broadcast
Hal Uplinger, Chairman, Doug Ivanovich, Vice-chairman; Daniel Dubie, Executive Producer

Gold Sponsors:

- Air Harbor Technologies
- Consuelo Zobel Alger Foundation
- Hawaiian Waters Adventure Park
- Hawaiian Children's Trust Fund
- Heal the World Foundation
- Hilton Hawaiian Village Hotel
- Mark Hughes, the Herbalife Family Foundation
- Rotary Club of Honolulu/District 5000
- Ronald McDonald House Charities
- Sheraton Waikiki Hotel
- Ultimate Innovations, Inc.

Silver Sponsors:

- AES Hawaii, Inc.
- Atlantis Adventures
- First Hawaiian Bank
- GEO Insights
- Gannet Foundation/Honolulu Advertiser
- Indiana Foundation
- Liberty House
- The Mendelson Family
- Government of Norway
- Shad Foundation
- Teen Connect
- Atherton Family Foundation
- Christel de Haan Foundation
- Foodland Supermarket Ltd.
- Hawaii Community Foundation
- Hey Jude! Inc.
- Kualoa Ranch
- McInerny Foundation
- Millennium Television Network
- Outrigger Hotels Hawaii
- Sogetsu Hawaii
- Waikiki Beachcomber Hotel

Bronze Sponsors:
- Ala Moana Hotel
- Bank of Hawaii
- The Cole Family Foundation
- Hard Rock Cafe
- Home Depot
- Ilikai Hotel
- Fred Matser Harmony/Fred Foundation
- Pepsi-Cola Hawaii
- Royal Dutch Shell
- R. Dwayne & Marti Steele
- Towill Tractors, Inc.
- Whale Song
- Amway Corporation
- BearCom Wireless Worldwide
- Eastman Kodak
- Hawaiian Airlines
- Honolulu Cellular
- Island Heritage
- Pacific-Beach Hotel
- Prince Hotels
- Sprint Hawaii
- Sub-Zero Distributors, Inc.
- United Airlines
- Youth Development Project

Cecilie Smith, our indefatigable office manager

VOLUNTEERS *The following great people gave of their time to create the Congress:*

Honorary Chair of the Hawaii Host Committee:
US Senator Daniel Inouye

Interntational Steering Committee:
Geoffrey Lipman *(chair)*
Arthur Gillette
David Wardrop
Kitty Ann
Debbie Simmons

Alex Achimore
Carl Ackerman
Amy Anderson
Don Anderson
State Representative Dennis Arakaki
Lloyd Asato
Vickie Asato
Mark Au
Koa Avery
Tom Barlow
Nancy Barry
Dixie Belcher
Sue Berg
Doc (Paul) Berry
Martha Black
Alfonso Braggs
Satoru Brooks
Grace Alvaro Caligtan
State Senator Suzanne Chun-Oakland
Linda Coble
Marilyn Cristofori
Karen Cross
Jeri Cvitanovich-Dubie
Jennifer Dang
Denise Davies
Edouard de Chateaubriand
Nancy Deeley
Lina Doo
Dick Dubanoski
Daniel Dubie
Bob Dye
Matt Fleming
Dolores Foley
Jim Gatti
Dorothy Goldsborough
Gig Greenwood
Carlene Gumapac
Kathy Harrington
Bellamann Hee, Jr.
Wayne Higa
Lacey Hilliard
Stanley Hong
Karen Hoshino
Tracy Janowicz
Arthur Jokela
Charles Kapua
Barbara Kelley
Christina Kemmer
Cynthia Kendlinger
Lonnie Kirby
Kiyoshi
Barbara Kuljis
Susan Kunisaki
Mieko Kuromiya
Brook Lee
Harvey Lee
Toni Lee
Kathy Leitheiser
Paul LeMahieu
Kainoa Li
Lynn Madden
Ann Malo
Makia Malo
Valerie Mariano
Lisa Maruyama
Mary Matayoshi
Carolyn Matsuda
Marika McCauley
Kat McDivitt
Gilbert Mendelson
Manuel C. Menendez III
Bruce Miller
Joan Naguwa
Clara Olds
Debra Olson
Colonel Orlan Peterson
Diane Phillips
Sam Powell
Josh Reppun
Veronika Rose

Representative Brian Schatz
Jennifer Sceifo
Ann Schmeisser
Kalena Silva
Gary Siracusa
Donovan Slack
Cecile Smith
John Spicola
Muriel Spicola
Karen Street
Lowell Strombeck
Jon Sugai
Mary Sugiyama
Vicky Suyat
Joanne Tachibana
Tiny Tadani
State Representative K. Mark T Takai
Adele Tasaka
C.L. Thames
Paul Tuan Tran
Lt. Sean Tsuha
Michelle Turner
Gary Uyeda
Lynn Watanabe
Sister Malia Wong
Beatrice Yamasaki
Ian Yee

YOUTH SUPER STEWARDS
We thank the Ke ala Hoku program of the Hawaii Community Services Council for arranging this team of excellent young people who helped organize the Congress:

Director: Rob James

Tae Ho Su
Mele Sax-Barnett
Kris Okazaki
Leanne NaKamura
Myles Javillonar
Isaac Kern
Jolyn Campbell
Jessica Countess
Pono Ordonez
Adrian Carmichael
Pattie Cabrido
Shanna Woolbright
Jeannie Pinpin

Theresa Engel
Jayne Shimamura
Mary Ann Feceido
Karani Burgess

HOST FAMILIES In their evaluations of the Congress, 90% of delegates said staying with Hawaiian host families was a very positive part of the Congress. Mahalo to the following for opening your hearts and homes to the young leaders of the AYPC:

Alex & Judith Achimore
Agapito & Maggie Alejo
Julie Almoilova
Elena Bradunas Aglinskas
Duane & Sally Bartholomew
Rich & Diane Bartosik
William & Marilyn Beardsley
Erik & Patrice Belcher
Bonnie Blair
Jorge & Nora Blanco
Eugene & Deborah Bonifacio
Terry & Pamela Bosgra
Vinnie Brazell
William & Patti Brizee
Michael & Maile Broderick
Don & Sandi Brough
David & Carey Brown
Perry & Maily Bucao
Rogelio & Luz Bungcayao
Gary & Lora Burbage
Raymond & Kathleen Burt
Mae Bush
Bartolome & Liza Cabaccang
Joe & Susan Cabrejos
Anacabio & Profetiza Cabrido
Julio & Filipina Cabusas
Jeff & Jo Anne Carpenter
James & Olivia Castro
Farries & Cheryl Chappel
Don & Wyn Child
Connie Ching
Mimie Ching
George & Laura Christensen
Michael & Suzanne Chun-Oakland
John & Julie Ushio Clark

Youth Super Stewards — taking a break!

Zig & Rosemary Coffey
William & Amy Cunningham
John & Elko Cusick
Genaru & Claudia Dadoy
Jon & Beth Davidann
Mark & Betsy Denzer
Hugo & Cindy deVries
Ned & Ann Dewey
Alfred & Sianing Domingsil
Jerry & Maureen Donerkeil-Bird
Daniel & Jeri Dubie
Mike & Abby Eaton
Stephen & Natalie Edwards
Dirk & Julie Elting
John & Barbara Engel
Michael & Mary Ennis
Robert & Janine Fairley
Chenoa Farnsworth
Derek Ferrar & Mary Roney
Peter & Christine Feldman
Sixto & Ofelia Fernandez
Virginia Fine
Ricardo & Rosario Francisco
Mike & Kay Fullerton
Ron & Dana Fujikake
Jay & Kathleen Fung
Cris & Lily Cabalo Galapon
Daniel & Flora Georgia
Joe & Kristine Giannasio
Steve & Suzanne Gilbert
Dingrena Gilo
Ramil Glauberman
Lorene Godfrey
Paul & Kammy Grable
Bob & Catherine Graham
Donald & Kay Graham
Dick Gushman
Robert Guyette & Melanie Ramones
Peter & Christine Feldman Hacker
Darin & Susan Haitsuka
Cliff & Nancy Halevi
David & Melinda Hamm
Clinton & Maki Hampton
David & Sally Hansen
Lee & Alicia Hanta
Kathy Harrington
Robert & Chula Harrison
James & Wendy Hayden
John & Emily Hawkins
Mark & Kim Hepburn
Jim & Darlene Hein
Richard Heyd
Roy & Carol Hiramoto
Kevin & Yvonne Hopkins
James & Margot Ige
Gladys Johnson
Michael & Susan Jones
Roger & Fe Jose
Cully Judd & Carol Silva
Randy & Jackie Kams
Kent & Elizabeth Keith
David & Gloria Kern
Ray & Dana King
Greg & Karen Knudson
Jaymark & Lori Komer

Doug & Joni Kroll
Bruce & Wendy Lagareta
Tom & Emily Laidlaw
Vince & Robin Lambert
Randy & Lorna Larson
Paul LeMahieu & Marina Piscolish
Andres Libed
Francis & Diana Lim
Victor & Anita Lim
Bob & Virginia Lippi
Wilson & Divinia Lucero
Carol Luke
Bud & Laurie Lush
Joyce Lyon
Alvin & Anne Maeda
Thomas & Mila Maglinao
Ronnie & Kathy Mahaffey
Fred Makinney
John & Carla Margenau
Alex & Elvira Mariano
Debra Martin
Rod & Jane Martin
Diane Mata
Eric & Purnima McCutcheon
Jim & Elizabeth McCutcheon
Kevin & Sherry McDougall
Richard & Windy McElroy
Robert & Debbie McWilliams
Rusty & Erlinda Meana
Stephen & Dorothy Meder
Yoshito & Emiko Miyashiro
Ken & Laxmi Moore
Ron & Cheri Moore
Oliver & June Morfit
Keala Morreira
Randall & Ramona Morris
Jacqueline Mossman
Paul & Fern Mossman
Bill & Jane Muench
Donnie & Mercedes Mullins
Stephen & Pat Murphy
Bruce & Elise Nacion
Grant & Peggy Nakamoto
Ravi & Synthis Sumukti Narayan
Kenneth & Brenda Nishimura
Timoteo & Esperanza Obrero
Creighton & Colette Oshiro
Andrew & Sandra Pak
Donald & Sally Parker
Craig Parkin
Richard & Candice Payne
John & Marjorie Penebacker
Dennis & Chandra Peters
Rob & Betty Perez
Bob & Cindy Perkins
Sarah Phillips
Jay & Brigitte Pierce
William & Magdelena Pinto
Leonid & Patti Poleshaj
Dennis & Christina Poma
Richard & Debra Pratt
James & Carrie Priest
Tom & Cher Prince
John Proud & Toni Worst
Craig Quick
Ruth Marie Quirk

Paul & Carol Quistgard
Stu & Vicky Ramil
Steve & Lyssa Reese
Gerald & Paula Reyes
Jeffrey & Sharalyn Richards
Ira & Karen Rohter
Jacqueline Rose
Brian & Mary Townsley Ross
Charley & Ida Sagadraca
Louis & Dell Salza
Felipe & Heide San Nicolas
Raymond & Rita Santana
Reggie & Carol Sayson
Van & Edith Shigemoto
Thom & Teri Simmons
Arlene Shimokawa
Saint-Clare & Charmaine Simpson
Barbara L. Smith
Jerry & June Smith
Mary Spellman
Norma Spencer
Allen & Liz Kam Steck
David & Gail Stein
Rick & Martha Stinton
Michael & Karen Street
Midge Strelow
Stan & Marina Sundlie
Hardja & JoLinda Susilo
Glenn & Wendy Taira
Ken & Esther Takemoto
Kelvin & Janice Taketa
Ted & Alice Talbott
Kimo & Ann Taylor
Heather Thiesse
Jim & Alyce Tipton
Paul & Libby Tomar
Mary Ann Tubin
Will & Lucy Tungol
Marcelino & Myrna Tupinio
David & Kirsten Turner
Roger & Margie Ulveling
Fred Unarce
Albert & Lorie Valencia
Michael & Joann Vickers
Linda Von Geldern
Greg & Rosa Wade
Wesley & Carrie Wakai
Jim & Marie Walsh
James & Mary Ann Wataru
Bradley & Helen Mary Wessel
Steve & Shelly White
Jim & Judy Wilkinson
Tom & Anne Williams
David & Jessica Wooley
Gary & Donna Wright
John & Jane Yanagida
Hsaeh-Wen & Ivy Yeh
Herman & Marcia Young
Mike & Nancy Young

MENTORS We thank the following for giving their time freely to advise the young people on their priorities:

Alani Apio
Doc (Paul) Berry
Orland Bishop
Tore Brevik
Ellen Brogren
Linda Buckley
LeVar Burton
Nanchy Davis Lewis
Sandy Davis
John Devaraj
Matilde Diaz-Armanaz
Richard Dubanowski
Daniel Dubie and Geri Cvitanovich-Dubie
Minerva Falcon
Dolores Foley
Samuel Gon
Werner Greis
Bani Dugal Gujral
Brien Hallett
John Harrison
Doug Ivanovich
Thomas Jackson
Noel Jacob Kent
Karl Kim
Daryl Kollman
Gertrude Kopyo
Mildred Kosaki
Leonard M. Kurz
Brett Leonard
Hunter Lovins
Makio Malo
Manuel C. Menendez III
Audrey Newman
Theodore Oben
Natasha Owen
Peter Raducha
Carlos Ravizza
Levana Saxon
Bo Shafer
Rosey Simonds
Jane Renfro Smith
Hanne Strong
Maurice Strong
Zehra Aydin Tsipos
Douglas Vincent
Cora Weiss
David Woollcombe

Aloha is both a greeting and a farewell. Literally it means the presence of the breath of life — "alo" meaning presence, "ha" means breath. (Hawaii literally means "breath on the water.") It is the defining word of Hawaiian culture: to "live aloha" means to show respect for all peoples, to care for them. Living aloha may be the best lesson we all learn from this Congress.

National Coordinators

We thank all those people and sponsors in each country who organised and supported the National Consultations. They were the backbone of this Congress and space alone dictates that we can name only some of them. In deep sadness, we acknowledge the participation of those in the countries marked with an asterisk (*) who, through the arbitrary whim of the US Consular officials who refused them visas, were unable to get their elected delegates to the Congress.

* Afghanistan
Rahela Hashim
UNCHS (Habitat)

* Albania
Andrian Vaso, AQUARIUS

* Algeria
Karim Boubred
Peace Child Algeria

Andorra
Jean-Michel Armengol
UNESCO Commisio Nacional

Argentina
Marina Mansilla Hermann
Mision Rescate Argentina
Sponsored by Comision de Asociados del Banco Credicoop; Sancor Cooperativas Unidas Ltd. Ing. Marcelo Dragan; Fundacion Ecologica por una Vida Mejor; Reynolds Argentina; Cican SA; Barbara Holzer(Energia Solar a Comun-idades Rurales); Ministerio de Educacion y Cultura de la Provincia de Jujuy; Legislatura de la Provincia de Jujuy; Ministerio de Gobierno de la Provincia de Jujuy; Diputado Guillermo Gloss; Agua de los Andes SA; Rio Uruguay Cooperat-iva de Seguros Ltda; Sindicato de Prensa de Entre Rios; Sr. Julio Rodolfo Solanas; Sr. Sergio Varisco; Honorable Camara de Diputados; Gobierno de la Provincia de Entre Rios; Excandelo Mega Disco; Sr. Eduardo Salerno; Leonardo Herlein

Armenia
Ashot Navasardyan
To Dr. Ruzanna Karapetyan we owe our deepest thanks ^ not only for hosting our National Consultation at her clinic but also for her wonderful example of humanitarian work that she does with every breath of her life; also many thanks to Mr. Vardan Navasardyan, the Director of the 21st Century Navasard Ltd, who provided free transportation to visit distant regions of Armenia;

Australia
Andrew Hudson
UNYA of Australia
Sponsored by Business Model Systems, Clifton Project Management, Campi Property Services Consumer Cashflow Promotions, Carey Baptist Grammar School, Wrixon House Pty.;

Austria
Dr. Werner Greis
United Games International

Azerbaijan
Azer Bairamov,
Sponsored by Ministry of Youth and Sports (Minister: Dr.Aboulfas Garayev); YOUTH DEVELOPMENT ORGANIZATION; AzEvroTel Joint Venture; BP/AMOCO; McCANN-Ericsson/Azerbaijan; Skylife TRAVEL;

Barbados
Reginald Burke
Caribbean Youth Environment Network
Sponsored by Caribbean Youth Envir-onment Network,Barbados Chapter; Barbados Youth Development Council; School for the Deaf and the Blind; Division of Youth Affairs - Government of Barbados; Ministry of Education; Ministry of the Environment, Energy and Natural Resources; Purity Bakeries Ltd.; Hanschell Inniss Ltd.; HYPE Magazine ;
The Barbados Advocate; Royal Bank of Canada; Tom Adams Financial Centre; Moore Paragon Ltd.; Barbados National Bank; Nick's Variety Discount

Belarus
Serge Balshakou
Sponsored by Belarussian Youth Entrepreneurship Support and Development Center

Belgium
Jo Van Cauwenberge
GREEN-Belgium

* Benin
Raymond Gbedo
Rescue Mission Benin

Bhutan
Narayan Katel
Society for Human Rights & Education in Bhutan

Bolivia
David Valdez, AJAYU
With thanks to: CEPA (Centro de Ecologia y Pueblos Andinos); Sari Stoops; Consejo de Municipio de Oruro; Colegio "Nacional Simon Bolivar" de Oruro; Colegio "Adela Zamudio" de Cochabamba; "AJAYU"; En Oruro a los chicos de la "Agenda 21" de Oruro, al Colegio "Mixto Bolivia"; Vice-ministerio de Asuntos de Genero y generacionales y a la Primera Dama de la Nacion

Brazil
Joao Camara, IBAMA,

* Cambodia
Yong Kim Eng, President, Khmer Youth Association
Sponsored by Samdech Hun Sen, Prime Minister of Royal Government of Cambodia; Khmer Youth Assoc.

* Cameroon
Daniel Ngungoh
Rescue Mission Cameroon

Canada
Susan Hawkins
Rescue Mission Canada
Sponsored by Government of Canada, Rotary Club of Huntsville; IMMA, Royal Canadian Legion, Lions Club; Superior Propane; Joggers Sports Store, The Painted Porch, Marlin Travel, Zellers Realty, World/Winterfold Muskoka Huntsville Place Mall, Robinson's Independent Grocers, Canadian Tire, Cavalcade Colour Lab, McDonald's, Jester's, Algonquin Outfitters, Cripple Creek Music, Village Shop, The Forester Press Ltd., The Bean, Nutty Chocolatier, Trinity United Church, 105.5 More FM, Reflections of Muskoka, Muskoka Bicycle, Kimberly-Clark Ltd; The Butcher's Daughters, Grandview Inn, Pasta Works, Blackburn's Landing, 103.5 Toronto, Joee-D Silver, Laurene Borley, Toronto Maple Leafs, The Toronto Blue Jays Baseball Team,
Enterprise Cape Breton, Bill Sibeon, Gisbert Wagner,

Colombia
Patricia Rojas and Jazmin Verdogo Aguilera

* Comoros
Ms. Sitti Fatouma Ahmed

Cook Islands
Maveni Kaufononga

Cote D'Ivoire
Degbedji Bruno

Czech Republic
Blanka Tomancokova,
UNESCO Club Olomouc

Denmark
Asser Mortensen

Dominica
Terry Orlando Raymond

Dominican Republic
Eugenio Sano Breton
Sponsored by Julio Cesar Lopez Diaz-Director, Equipo de Educacion Popular; Domingo Contreras, Director Direccion General de promocion de la Juventud; Divino Campusano- Contralor del Ayuntamiento del Municipio de Haina; Ines Maria Perez;

Ecuador
Jose Francisco Pereira

El Salvador
Marielos Bonilla, CESTA

Estonia
Kadi Bruus

* Ethiopia
Miss Mesmak Abebe

Finland
Ms. Viveka Nordman
Anja Kainu

* Gambia
Mr. Buramanding Kinteh
Sponsored by Tamba Dambell, Babucarr Cherno Jangwe, Assan Sowe

Ghana
Ebenezer Malcolm, Rescue Mission Ghana
Sponsored by Ashantin Gold Field Co. Ltd.; Ashantin Gold Field Schools; Grade Oduro, Isaac Kusi, Victor Arhin, Belinda Agbenyenu, Abena Ahenka, Dinah Antwi

Guyana
Trevor L. Benn

Honduras
Erick Castellanos
Consejo Nacional de la Juventud

Hong Kong
Mr. Charles Allison
YMCA's of Hong Kong

Hungary
Dr. Miklos Banhidi,
United Games Hungary

Iceland
Snorri Sigurdsson

India
Dr. S.N. Nair WWF-India,

Indonesia
Astri Rahayu Purnamawati
Ecoteens Club

Israel
Dina Jacobson
Peace Child Israel,
Sponsored by What If Foundation

Japan
Ms. Kazuyo Minamide
Osaka YMCA
Sponsored by All Nippon Airways Co. Ltd.; Osaka YMCA; National Council of YMCAs of Japan;

Jordan
Ahmad Rusan
The Royal Society for the Conservation of Nature

Kenya
Juma Assiago,
Home Planet - YMP,
Sponsored by United Nations Centre for Human Settlements (Habitat); Youth Director - Selman Erguden; Kenya Tourism Federation, Director: Jan Mohammed; Serena Hotels and Lodges Ltd.; Nation Newspapers, Director: Joe Adongo; Consolata Fathers Seed Studio and Magazine, Editor: Fr. Luigi Anataloni; The Nairobi City Council - Mayors Parlour Nakuru Municipal Council Local Agenda 21 Group; The Shelter Forum; The World Wild Life Fund (WWF)

* Korea
Ms. Ji Young Kang
Seoul YMCA

Kuwait
Tracey Hawkins

Kyrgyzstan
Gulnara Arnambetova

Latvia
Diana Shuga

* Lebanon
Abbas Zahreddine, President
Lebanon Nature Environment Association House of Env. & Sustainable Development

Lesotho
Mrs. Emily Makharile
Development for Peace Education (DPE)

Liberia
Mr. Richelieu M. Allison
Voice of the Future

Lithuania
Ruta Ivoskute
Lithuanian Youth Centre

Macedonia
Gjakush Kabashi
1st Children's Embassy
Sponsored by Travel agency "Orfej", Skopje

Madagascar
Ms. Bakolinirina Robertine
Sponsored by Ministry of Education: Mr Jacky Simon; Ministry of Environment: ONE (Office National pour l'Environnement); SOAM Tamatave: Tamatave 501, Madagascar; Association des Handicapés de Tamatave; Mr Nomentsoa Andriama- monjy; Rajoelinirina Jelice Houlder Alice; O.N.G Mahasoa Mr Le Chef de division Cons-eiller Pedagogique à l'EN2

Malawi
MacBain Mkandawire

Mali
Cheickne Lagdaf

Northern Marianas
John Oliver Gonzales

Mauritius
T.M.S. Futloo

Mexico
Luis Betanzos de Mauleon
Mision Rescate Mexico
Sponsored by Daimler Chrysler de Mexico S.A. de C.V.; SMURFIT Papel y Carton S.A. de C.V.; Programa de Naciones Unidas para el medio Ambiente; Oficina Regional para America Latina y el Caribe

Micronesia
Tanya Harris
Sponsored by Bank of Guam, External Affairs, FSM Supreme Court, Senator Rufin Micky, Senator Selestino Emwalu, Setiro Paul, Timothy Moses, Mr & Mrs Konno, Tiser Lipwe, Gabriel Olopwy, Chuuk Board of Education, Chuuk State Legislative Branch.

Mongolia
Ms. Burmaa Radnaa

Morocco
Guerraoui Driss
with many thanks to the Government of the Kingdom of Morocco.

Namibia
Connie Botma

Nepal
Urjana Shrestha

New Zealand
Neihana Jacob
Sponsored by Air New Zealand & Pakuranga College

Nicaragua
Elvira Blass

Niger
Benadetta Rossi
Sponsored by Soroptomists Intl.

* Nigeria
Chris N. Ugwu
Efiong J. Jacob
Rescue Mission Nigeria

Norway
Kjetil Hillestad,
UNA of Norway
Sponsored by Worldwide Adventures,
Erik Holm-Olsen, US Embassy, Oslo, Aircontact, UNA of Norway

Oman
Hassan Mushtaq Al Saleh
Sponsored by Gulf Air

Pakistan
Syed Abu Ahmad AKIF

Peru
Ivan Lanegra, Asociacion para Desarrollo Sostenible

Philippines
Mr. Crisologo Caparoso
Cebu YMCA

Qatar
Dana Shaddad
Sponsors: Qatar Intl. School; Darwish Travel Bureau/KLM Royal Dutch Airlines

Russia
Valentina Ivanova,
Peace Child Rzhev Group

Rwanda
Aaron Turamye

* Senegal
Souleymane Diop
Mission Terre Senegal

Seychelles
Miss Jeanette Larue
Colibri Wildlife Club
Sponsored by Dutch Trust Fund for Seychelles; Air Seychelles; State Assurance Corporation; Seychelles Breweries; Seychelles Children's Fund; Seychelles Broadcasting Corporation; Minister Danny Faure of Education

Sierra Leone
Sheku Syl Kamara
Peace Child Sierra Leone

Singapore
Melissa Aratani Kwee
PAX (Project Access)

Slovakia
Katarina Labasova

Slovenia
Ms. Anita Stefin

South Africa
Margaret Bennett
Girl Guides Association of RSA
Sponsored by Nanbithi Rotary Club, Ladysmith Town Council and Community of Ladysmith; Anglo American Corporation; Sunstove Organisation

Spain
Manuel A. Fernandez

Sri Lanka
Dinesh Weerakkody

* Sudan
Mrs. Salwa Tabiedi

* Swaziland
Bhekie Patson Metfula
Sponsored by UNICEF Office - Mbabane Swaziland; Ministry of Education - Swaziland; American Cultural Centre, Swaziland; Swaziland Youth Forum

Tanzania
Colin Kajisi,
Amani UNESCO Club,

Taiwan
Mr. David Chang
The YMCA of Taiwan

Thailand
Ms. Naruemol Kunanugool

* Tibet
Wangchuk Tsering

* Tonga
Valerie Thompson

Trinidad & Tobago
Soloman Aguillera

Turkey
M. Orhan Efe
Local Agenda 21 Bursa
With thanks to: the Munic-ipality of Greater City of Bursa; Ta- High School, Bursa; Nova Ca-da Fen Preparatory Course Centre, Bursa; Uluda Gazoz Corp., Bursa; Guekrue Sankay, Bursa; AMWAY, Tuerkiye Corporation, Izmir; Sueta Corporation; Aktar Lastik Industrial Corp.; Turan Tayan; Turkish Airlines, Istanbul; Local Agenda 21, Bursa; Meditour Tourism Agency, Istanbul; Savcan Textiles; Contitech Lastik; Kafkas Pasta Lekerleme; Euro Trans Corp.;

Uganda
Bakyayita Jasper
Rescue Mission Uganda

Ukraine
Peter Leemar
Peace Child Ukraine
Sponsored by Minister the Cabinet of Ministers of Ukraine, Anatoly Tolstoukhov, Tatiyana L. Hohlova, Ukrainian Youth Agency, Director: Natalya Schelkunova; Parents' Aid in Favour Fund of Kiev Valery Molchnov Lyceum 138; Eastern-Ukrainian Youth Organizations Union

United Kingdom
Lissa Wheen, PCI,
Sponsored by Queen Anne Street Educational Trust; Dill Faulkes Educational Trust; Bolton Borough Council; Access Communications UK Ltd., St Joan of Arc School, Rickmansworth, The Davison Family; Fairbridge; Salford & 42nd Street; Plymouth City Council, Surfers Against Sewage, Stead & Simpson, The Body Shop, Plymouth Environment Forum, Kings Bench Chambers, Combe Dean School, Eggbuckland Community College, Mr Finn, Eggbuckland Labour Group, Plymouth Girls Brigade; Prudential and The London Borough of Camden; Global News Education Trust and the family and friends of all!

United States of America
Erin Mendelson

Uzbekistan
Gulamova Bonu

Viet Nam
Ha Lan Anh

* Yemen
Ahmed Al-Sayaghi

Zambia
Shalala Oliver Sepiso

Zimbabwe
Leonard Kachingwe
Rescue Mission Zimbabwe
Sponsored by Zimbabwe Sugar Refineries; Zesk Industries - Harare; Scotfin - Harare; Stanbic Bank, Nelson Mandela Ave, Harare; First Merchant Bank, Samora Machel Ave, Harare; Reserve Bank Of Zimbabwe; Anglo American Bank; Air Harbour Technologies; Astra Paints; Zimbabwe Sun Ltd; Speciss College, Harare

Delegates & Activists

Afghanistan
Samira Mahbuob
Zuhra Bahman

Andorra
Pryia Gurmukhani
Xavier Vilana

Argentina
Leandro Ahl
Leandro Hernan Deheza
Tamara Parma
Octavio Wehr
Walter Rodriquez
Ileana Pacher
Natalia Florenza
Facundo Maggioli
Sacha De Napoli
Jeronimo Maggioli
Victor Manuel Perez
Ivana Ferrarese
Miriam Morales
Cristian Javier Braga
Julio Cesar Lorenzo
Lucia Edelstein
Maria Laura Alvarez
Ludmila Losi
Vanesa Maria Pressel
Veronica Falcon
Federico Panzieri
Gaston Santoiani
Sofia Cibert
Rosana Kolmaier
Silvia Estela Aramayo
Carlos Juan Osman
Cecilia Monnittola
Marina Hermann

Armenia
Davit Dallakyan
Karen Sarkavagyan

Australia
Ishaan Nangia
Mia Handshin
Louisa May Kirby

Austria
Daniela Wilding
Annemarie Schlack
Raimund Blaser

Azerbaijan
Luedtke Konul aliyeva
Narquiz Damirli
Orkhan Azayen
Rustam Alekperon
Teymur Jafarov
Nazrin Garayeva
Elchin Huseynzade
Gadir Aliyev
Elchin Gazanfarov
Sahil Babayev
Lala Rustamova
Taliboa Jamil

Barbados
Neysa Sabrina Ford
Philip Alan Toppin

Belarus
Hanna Balshakova
Dzimtry Savelau
Siarhei Balshakova

Belgium
Joris Claeys
Joris Van der Leest
Delphine Hesters

Benin
Mylene Deleke
Eugene Adjovi

Bhutan
Robi Gurun
Samar Samal

Bolivia
Abigail Espinoza
Danae Aguilar
Carlos Paredes
Humberto Cespedes
Randolf Pinaya

Bosnia/Herzegovina
Irfan Polimac
Katarina Ceranic

Brazil
Isabel Pereira
Poema Costa
Roberta Benazzi

Cameroon
Peter Nyoh
Daniel Ngungoh

Canada
Ali McDonnell
Melanie Coulas
Karen McKnight
Michelle Luxon
Devon Gillis
Garnet Smith
John Jardine
Jamie Sealy
Stephanie MacDonald
Christopher Waddington
Sandra Melbourne
Genia Melbourne
Bevan Wilson
Matthew Clarke
Tyler Lane
Zoe Hawkins

Colombia
Laura Jimenez
Francisco Perrera

Cook Islands
John Vano Vano
Nukutau Pokura

Cyprus
Louis Loizou
Maria Elena Anatassiades

Czech Republic
Martin Sin
Blanka Tomancakova
Jan Sojka
Michaela Appeltova
Jan Slunsky
Jindrich Husicka

Denmark
Asser Mortensen
Sebastian Hansen

Dominican Republic
Yoselin Santiago
Eleuren Mendez

Domenica
Edith Williams
Marvin Marie

Ecuador
Nicolas Cabanilla
Andrea Carpio Penafiel
Giselle Martinez
Jose Moncayo
Maria Arboleda
Lorena Gutierrez

El Salvador
Maria Bonilla
Paty Pleitez
Sofia Bares Rivas

Estonia
Jorge Palma
Madis Masing
Maria Savisaar

Ethiopia
Amanuel Abay
Redient Abebe

Finland
Kristoffer Othman
Riika Blomqvist
The Gambia
Famara Singata

Ghana
Fidelia Adomako-mensah
Dominica Owiredu
Hannavi Pabby
George Williams

Guyana
Lennox Caleb
Beatrice Quagraine
Francess Legall
Gordon Mosley

Honduras
Grace Dubon
Griselda Linares Banegas

Hong Kong
Chris Chan

Hungary
Edina Papp

Iceland
Snorri Sigurdsson
Melkorka Olafsdottir

India
Astha Gupta
Taarika Chopra
Dhruv Malhotra
Bani Dugal Gujral
Anika Singh
Purnima Datt
Vichitra Rajasingh
Kuheli Bhattacharya
Madhurjya Phukan
Sujay Swadi Sanan
Tharun James

Indonesia
Ayi Nurwandi
Chitra Lestari

Israel
Avivit Kodgia
Essam Doad

Japan
Kazuyo Minamide
Mai Domae
Miki Mita
Nishio Sanae
Shiho Fujimaru
Daisuke Kurokawa
Hiroyuki Fukui

Jordan
Rada Halaseh
Ahmad Madadha

Kenya
Olivia Nyambura
Michelle Abok
Alfred Kumboto
Murugi Maina Carol
Juma Assiago
Nick Mutavi
Susan Ngugi

Korea
Kyung-Hoon Lee
Paul Chung

Dong-Hyun Choi

Kuwait
Karim Alaa El Assal
Lillian Gabra Fam

Kyrgyzstan
Elena Tregoubova
Temirbek Altimishov

Latvia
Ineta Reinvalde
Ingus Zalitis

Lesotho
Ruben Makoae
Lerato Matlosa

Liberia
Felicia Kai
Octawie Moore
Benjamin Sanvee
Ernest Subah
Richelieu Allison
Stacey Mason
A. Leemu Clark
L. Kevin Johnson
Doreen Ellis

Lithuania
Andrej Afanasjevas
Lokas Salasevicius
Evaldas Klimas
Eva Giedrimaite
Cristina Baubinaite
Daiva Petkeviciute
Egle Butkute
Lugile Balzekaite
Solveiga Skendelyte
Civile Kelpsaite
Elena Bradunas Aglinskas

Macedonia
Ile Jandreska
Gjakush Kabashi

Madagascar
Lovanirina Andrianilana
L. Andriamamonjy

Malawi
Caleb Gondwe
Teema Buleya

Mali
Picko Abdoul Wahab
Drame Nima
Comb Goita
Lokiatou Kone

N. Marianas
Franklin Palacios
Earl King-Nabors
Lamona Concepion

Mauritius
Tushrina Futloo
Nadeem Dilloo

Mexico
Annette Richaud
Mariana Romero
Eduarco Lisker
Roberto Alvarez
Ana Ortega
Luis Betanzos de Mauléon
Mario Cabal

Micronesia
Moses Veracruz
Vanessa Kanno

Mongolia
Tuvshinjargal Nomondelger
Erdene Davaakhuu

Morocco

Foukahi El Avadh
Omar Lemsoui
Fadi a Halfi
Imare El Bekali
Ayuud El Aasi
Azeccine Dahloumi
Behai Mememe
Chafika Afac
Kanll Raihen
Rkia Achmel
Hicham Grine
Leila Larbus
Sasan Bekesmi
Younes Sektouri
Youssef Bouabid
Dalia El Kortobi
Rouri Dafia
Kawtar Bermavm
Sara El Fandi

Namibia
Antoine Smith
Monica do Santos
Henri Snargua
Michael Merag

Nepal
Ashish Beval
Bithuri Eaneth
Srijana Shrestha
Urane Sarestha

New Zealand
Melissa James
Chris Shaw

Nicaragua
Emmanuel Lope
Engel Sauu Coregon

Niger
Mrie Le Mignon
Mohammel Backar
Ahmed Abubumaye

Norway
Iselin Stensdal
Ola Assanli Rokkones

Omar
Sara Majeed Al Asfoor
Hassan Mushteq Al Saleh

Pakistan
Sidra Iqbal
Rabia Mir
Madiha Desmuth
Khurram Jumali

Peru
Leticia Martinez
Ursula Carrascal
Francisco Villalcos

Philippines
Archie Cruz
Jose Fauro Varela
Xavier Golea
Karma Eora
Michelle Dadiuc
Francis Contcemino
Juman Devere

Qatar
Lairy Isa
Mammen Tharakan
Lara Kopt
Renza Monte
Shadi Odeh
Uday Rosero
Reen Snaudad

Russia
Anastasia Kotlora
Antonia Dovogov
Ioulia Hocethkova

be the change

93

Rwanda
Jannet Tumusenga
Aaron Turamye

Senegal
Souleymane Diop

Seychelles
Sharon Isaac
Roger Lawen

Sierra Leone
Mustafa Massaquoi
Justina Kamara
Sheku Kamara

Singapore
Candice Wang Pei Ying
Tham Jian Yang Sam
Linda Ismail
Nadya Melic
Tan Jun Hao Eugene

Slovakia
Peter Fila
Stanislava Homolova
Veronika Skodova

Slovenia
Anita Stefin
Darja Janjatovic
Helena Klanjscek
Jana Jarc
Matez Khep
Masa Borisov
Ziga Vavpotic
Lucka Lihteneger
Jelka Fric

South Africa
Bushra Razack
Caroline Mokotong
Jacqueline Bischof
Nina Kettle
Yolande Van Rensburg
Dlamini Clement

Spain
Carmen Fernandez
Melina Martinez

Sri Lanka
Dinesh Weerakkody
Noeline Perera

Swaziland
Pascale Paiva
Sicolelwe Haltshwayo

Taiwan
Feng-Yi Hsiao
Lily Tseng
Nei-chien Chang
Kaita (Alen) Wei
Leann Hung
Lee Yin-chin
Chen Li-Yen
Hsing Yun Hsu
Yen-Hsi (Nancy) Chen
Yi Ping (Betina) Lee
Yuan Yu-Tsing
Tseng Feng-Yi
Tsai Pei-Yin
Chu Chun-Chang
Chen Hsiang-mei
Tsai Sui-Ju

Tanzania
Fadhulun Mohamed
Joyce Shabani
Agather Muweno
Jane Mary Ruhundua
Abeid Mtezo
Deogratius Rutta
Bonus Caesar
Murtaza Tharos
Ritha Mwamanga

Thailand
Chutatip Chitpromphan
Nithinan Nakkarin
Peera Kasemtanakul
Saravuth Ruangsutham
Pimporn Thungkasmvathana

Tonga
Michael Koloi
Ebonie Chal Fifiti

Trinidad & Tobago
Shamfa Cudjoe
Rocky Aguillera

Turkey
Ayse Ozgumus
Kemal Uysal
Yasemin Ozge Tezel
Defne Cizakea
Nihal Karagoz
Gokhan Alan
Kadir Karalar
Gozde Boga
Sennur Delibas
Onder Kas'kc'lar
Tlgim Dara
Bahadir Katikol
Tarik Akyol
Ugur Bayulgen

Uganda
Evelynn Hantale
Ivan Karuma

Ukraine
Peter Lymar
Volodymyr Nemertsalov
Dmytro Donets
Alesya Savchenko
Ganna Kokoza
Olena Ukhanova

United Kingdom
Katy Beinart
Anthony Booth
William Masters
Stephanie Illingworth
Susanna Hill
Betty Berhane
Elizabeth Wood
Daniel Keogh
Iman Fadaei
Jenny Rowe
Rheillyn Valdez
Colin Bell
Ian Davies

United States of America
Malachie Hull
Alison Sokol
Michael Sokol
S. Seng
Jennifer M. Ryan
Komsan Say
Manny Sitthixay
Sergio Villa
Jessica Countess
Jill Borges
Matt Hammond
Melissa Maggiori
Jesse Lowers
Elissa Hoots
Cassie Neilsen
Justin Wasylczuk
Felicia Dubie
Danielle Richardson
Kara Bakie
Katie McCarthy
Kai Saint John
Melana Yanos
Jayanti Nand
Daniel Beebe
Fiona Wainwright

Colin McCormick
Joel Mateo
Lisa Williams
Timofey Orcharenko
Nina Mirani
Ja'hae Davies
Benjamin Quinto
Toby Matz
Jasmyn Leonard
Jeremy Roske
Chrysta Olson
Kaitlyn Olson
Ian Marstrand
Rashaun Marstrand
Matou Marstrand

Uzbekistan
Mavlanjon Mukhitdinov
Diyora Mahmudova

Vietnam
Pham Thi Thu Huong
Vu Thuy Anh

Yemen
Mohammed Fakher

Yugoslavia
Livia Sari

Zambia
Brian Kanswe
S. Sepiso
Janet Mwafulirwa

Zimbabwe
Esther Mazhande
Farai Chipato
Geoffrey Martin
Gordon Shirto
Shana Watermeyer
Hillary Tsumba
Jeanette Williamson
Anusha Jogi
Jaensch Masanga

Artists Groups:

Imbongwe Dancers, Zimbabwe:
Sponsored by Air Habour Technologies Ltd.
Albert Nyath
Peter Dhlowo
Sandile Mpande
Bigboy Sibanda
Tendai Mudimu
Nickson Nkomo
Clement Dlomo
Pretty Sithole
Zimazile Mguni
Siphathiwe Moyo
Memory Muzondo

Eastern All Stars, Azerbaijan:
S. Adigozalova
L Alekperova
N Ibrahimova
L. Khanizada
S Panahova
N Parvindi
N Mammadzada
S Abasova
Anil Mamedov
H. Mamedov
U Khanifayeva
G Nazrin
T. Jamil
M Sevinj

Cecinka Dance Group, Slovakia:
Andelova Jana
Antalova Anna
Balanova Zuzana
Brachtlova Anna
Bakkaiova Tatiana
Hanusova Nina
Hanusova Julia
Miklovieova Maria
Marcilinova Zuzana
Svobodova Petronela
Piczekova Anna
Rilova Michaela
Vitkova Katarina
Eepec Jan
Gazdik Matu
Kolenie Igor
Lieskovsky Libor
Mezei Miroslav
Pucovsky Luka
Vejeik Matu

SANGIA, Canada:
Sandra Melbourne
Genia Melbourne

Young Reporters:
Alexander Woollcombe (UK)
Bremley Lyngdoh (India)
Paula S. Magalhaes (Brasil)
Gregor Novak (Slovenia)
Kip Oebanda (Philippines)
Ernesto J Vargas (Costa Rica)
Foukahi Elmedi (Morocco)
Bouabid Youssef (Morocco)
Belkasmi Sarah (Morocco)
Nawal El Harim (Morocco)
Ayoub El Aiassi (Morocco)
Leila Laroussi (Morocco)
Tom Burke (UK)
Amy Saunders (UK)

Ohana:
Family/community. 'Oha' means to grow, thrive, expand. Hawaiians profoundly honor family values. By using the same word for communities, they extend the same values to neighbours, friends - indeed the whole family of living things on earth. We recognise a big and thriving Ohana in all the people listed here.

Regional Priorities

The Congress called for young people to determine priorities for the new Millennium. In setting the task, we were well aware that issues are interconnected and interdependent. But most Congress delegates agreed it was important for young people to think about where global attention should be focused first. One said: "You can't wear your five favorite sets of clothes at the same time. You have to choose one!" Another delegate explained: "If there is a room full of people, one has to be the first through the door." In that spirit, Congress delegates conducted a secret ballot to set their priorities. They were counted by seeing which TEN priorities were mentioned most often. We then divided that total by the sum of the placings to get an average position. These are the global priorities:

Global Position:	Priority:	Average Position(1-10):	Total No. of Mentions:
1	Education	1.654	329
2	Peace	2.117	222
3	Environment	2.956	294
4	Human Rights	3.352	258
5	Corruption	3.417	48
6	Poverty	3.443	203
7	Health	3.818	214
8	Population	3.897	58
9	Democracy	3.786	14
10	Economy	4.070	43

Africa

To many, Africa is just a developing continent. What people don't focus on are the different rates at which countries are developing. Africa's development is diverse, and priorities differ completely from shore to shore. This caused problems in the regional discussions, as people were fighting about which priority was most important in their country — not which was the most important for the whole continent. This was the result of the democratic vote:

Education
Poverty
Peace
Human rights
Corruption

Asia

In the Asian region meeting there was heated debate over the most important issues — overpopulation, education, poverty, and human rights. It was realized that solutions to the priorities agreed upon were mutually reinforcing. For example, if there was effective population control, it would help in delivering education to more people, and vice versa. Other important issues descussed were the ill treatment of women and child labor. After much discussion, the following priorities were agreed upon, here listed in order of importance.

Education
Environment
Peace
Poverty
Human rights

Europe

Europe's regional priorities reflect the diversity and mix of cultures. Discussions were heated, to say the least. But we all agreed that, wherever we live, education is the most important priority for change. We also rated peace and human rights high, as parts of Europe are still plagued by war.

Education
Environment
Human rights
Peace
Health

Is the world ready for a global flag? Many beautiful designs were submitted for consideration. However, Congress youth decided that the world is not yet ready for a global flag. "How can the world be united under one flag?" they asked. What do you think? For more info: www.globalflag.net

Island States

Delegates from small island nations were very organized and had no problem coming up with priorities for their nations.

It is a very diverse group, made up of nations from around the world including Trinidad and Tobago, the Dominican Republic, Madagascar, Seychelles, Mauritius, Northern Marianas, Tonga, Australia, New Zealand, and others.

Besides the top priorities below, delegates discussed unemployment, peer counseling programs, hunger, and domestic violence. It was decided that some of these areas could be solved if top priorities such as the economy and human rights were addressed.

Education, especially environmental education
Sustainable resources
Management
Human rights and conflict resolution
Health
Sustainable economic development

Latin America

Puff! I still can't believe that we came up with a list of regional priorities! I thought it would never happen for we discussed them over and over. Somehow, that makes me happy. It demonstrates that we are all committed.

We chose education as our top priority. For us, it is like the trunk of a tree from where the other branches sprout. Both the trunk and the branches depend on each other. For that reason you can think of these as investments. Education would be a long-term investment but, to make sure that it will produce its fruits in the future, you have to invest in stopping corruption, preserving the environment, improving health, and assuring human rights for all, in the present.

Dominique Mansilla Hermann, Argentina

Education
Corruption
Environment
Health
Human rights

North America

When we were asked to decide on our order of priorities, we were presented with a point of view. When we realized that, around the world, there are many different ratings for priorities and all of them are "first" somewhere, we stopped fighting over numbers and got down to thinking what we could do about them. All need to be addressed simultaneously for any progress to be made. They are interrelated so that one cannot be dealt with without the others.

We envision them as a circle or sphere. There are unlimited beginnings and endings. If one is missing, the circle is broken and nothing can be solved.

If you like the image of priorities leaving a room one at a time, suggesting that one has to be first, we suggest, "Make a bigger door!" Only in that way can we make synergies between the solutions to these different global problems.

Education
Environment
Poverty
Human rights
Health

"A Small Planet"
Nadezhda Porozhnaya, 14, Russia

ETERNAL LIFE
CHURCH OF GOD IN CHRIST
PH. 808-621-0955
BISHOP JOSEPH BOOKHART
PROPHETESS H.M. BOOKHART
PO BOX 2738
MILILANI, HI 96789

TO: "K.J." "God Bless You"
From: Moma and Poppa Bookhart
June 18, 2014

"Happy Childhood"
Victoria Pristup, 14, Russia